ISBN 978-0-578-09085-6

Published by Auxano Press
Tigerville, South Carolina
www.AuxanoPress.com

Worth Its Weigl

A Collection of Tith
from Past Pres
of the Pastors' Co
of the Southern Baptis

Edited by John I

Auxano
PRESS

Tigerville, South Ca
www.AuxanoPress.

CONTENTS

FOREWARD

About fifty years ago, Southern Baptist leaders launched a stewardship emphasis called "Every Baptist a Tither." It didn't result in *every* Baptist becoming a tither, but it was a step in the right direction. Its sentiment was right. In fact—more than sentiment—its theology was right. The Bible teaches that God expects His work to be cared for by the faithful tithing of His people. "The tithe belongs to the Lord!"

How are we doing today? Not as good as we ought. Not as good as the past. Studies reveal that the average gift of Baptists to their churches is barely over 2%. Hardly a tithe. During what is arguably the most affluent period of our history, American Christians, including Baptists, are giving a smaller percent of their income to their churches than the people of the Great Depression of the 1930s.

Additionally, the Barna Group released poll results from early 2011 indicating the number of tithers among American adults (to any church or charity) dropped to 4%. The average had been 5-7% the last decade (*World*, June 4, 2011). It has been estimated that had only the *active* membership of our Baptist churches tithed last year, total church income would have more than doubled. More than $10 billion of tithes were left in the pockets of Baptist church members while God's ministries across the world went lacking.

Every pastor has the duty and the opportunity to develop the principles and practices of stewardship among his members. How satisfying and meaningful it is each time a Christian family learns to "bring the tithe into the storehouse."

This book contains messages in the area of Biblical stewardship by some of our most capable pastors. Our prayer is that the fruit of their efforts to see their flocks "grow in the grace of giving" will aid you as you pursue that same worthy pastoral responsibility among your own people.

David E. Hankins

Executive Director,
Louisiana Baptist Convention

INTRODUCTION

Charles H. Spurgeon, the prince of preachers said, "*The power that is in the gospel does not lie in the eloquence of the preacher, otherwise men would be the converters of souls. Nor does it lie in the preacher's learning, otherwise it would consist in the wisdom of men. We might preach until our tongues rotted, till we would exhaust our lungs and die, but never a soul would be converted unless the Holy Spirit be with the Word of God to give it the power to convert the soul.*"

Perhaps like no one else, preachers understand the fire in their hearts – their calling to lead people to the truth. Ultimately, the desire of the preacher is to facilitate the work of God's Holy Spirit in the lives of people for salvation and lordship. When the truth about lordship is preached, the faithful man must confront the Scriptures relating to the realm of financial accountability. You cannot dodge the bullet. You must preach the Word and let the Holy Spirit do His best work at transforming the souls of men and women.

Not that long ago I heard the old revivalist Leonard Ravenhill ask a poignant question, "*Is there not a prophet among us?*" Is there someone who has the prophet's mantel on them to confront the church and the culture with the timeless truths of God's Word? Will that prophet proclaim the whole counsel of God? Or has the contemporary preacher limited himself to the areas of life that are more palatable to the culture? Has preaching become the "really big show" for one's Sunday morning lineup? Is there the possibility of one crying in the wilderness, "The day of the Lord is at hand!"?

But it is so hard to be bold in our preaching when the people we are attempting to lead and disciple are pushing back on last Sunday's sermon with a complaint or an innuendo. As a result, have we turned our focus away from those truths that are too uncomfortable, too strident, too disciplined, too hard for today's metro-man who thinks the world revolves around what he wants? In the preacher's quest for a relevant message, have we found ourselves embracing pop culture, pop psychology and pop leadership principles?

So when was the last time, the designated prophet of God stepped into his assignment and said, "Thus saith the Lord…" regarding finances? And he did so not because the church was behind on its budget or there was some special need. He spoke as one with authority from the Lord with a message from the Word burning in his soul. He preached as if he were Gideon dismantling the high places of the cultural gods.

Where do faithful preachers find the encouraging resources to embolden their faith? They are out there. When you find a resource or sermon from a faithful effective prophet of God, you will find that His message leaps across generational and sub-culture demographics. For those who are spiritually hungry, His message is worth its weight in gold.

This is a collection of sermons by the presidents of the Southern Baptist Pastors' Conference. Each man is a clear communicator of God's Word. One of the reasons they were elected by their fellow Southern Baptist pastors is that they are really good preachers. They are each respected for their private devotion and their public desire to obey God rather than man. You will note in each sermon there is no manner of wishy-washy theology. Each man preaches passionately the Word of God. They do so unashamed and with authority. They speak as one voice that Jesus Christ must be Lord of all!

It doesn't take rocket science to look at what is most important to the western culture. It's the economy. It's our personal finances. It's our stuff, gadgets, conveniences, vacations, credit cards, pets or favorite sport. Whatever we invest the most time and resources in is most likely what's most important to us.

Don't we think God has something to say about finances and the stuff we call ours? Sure He does. He also is quite aware of how He planted us here in the balance between allegiances so that we will by faith choose HIM above all else. As followers of the Lord Jesus, we are called to receive the principles of His Word and affirm them by faith and practice. This includes the principles of finance and personal stewardship.

Believers desperately need the faithful prophet of God to stand up and preach the Word of God in power and authority. We need the prophet of God's message so that the people of God will cast down allegiances to the financial gods and declare with one voice that Jesus Christ is Lord of all, not Lord of some.

Indisputably, Scott Preissler, director of the Center for Biblical Stewardship at Southwestern Baptist Theological Seminary, possesses the largest library in the world on the subject of biblical stewardship. He believes there has been a conccrtcd attack against Christian giving over the course of an entire generation. In a quote from *Perspectives on the Tithe* by David A. Croteau, Preissler said the following:

> Amongst a seeming epidemic of "affluenza" or affluence in our materialistic culture, there seems also to exist amnesia by pastors that teaching about giving and stewardship are related to church survival, growth, and spreading the gospel locally, nationally and internationally. Stewardship remains the once-a-year sermon for most pastors, who seem afraid to deliver this biblical teaching to their local church members.

A once-a-year homily is not sufficient to help people capture the Lordship of Christ, especially in the private realm of personal financial realities. We seem to have trouble grasping that part of making fully devoted followers. Why? Because it involves preaching, teaching and our personal life message about how we, the preachers, are both disciplined and openhanded with our dollars and assets.

Living according to financial biblical principles is so uncommon in this culture. A dedicated Christian layman and I were out visiting people in a new subdivision of the Dallas/Fort Worth Metroplex. As we walked from one house to the next house, he said something that captured my thinking. "Pastor, we must pray for these people that live out here because most of them live in a house of cards." He was spot on.

How many homes in that one subdivision are up for foreclosure because someone missed one paycheck or because of an unanticipated emergency? How many are spending 110% of their take home pay every week? How many owe credit card companies more than the equity of their houses? And we are going to encourage these people to tithe?

We witnessed and started winning a few to Christ. Then we began to teach them how to live disciplined lives before the Lord. And for the majority, their financial obligations were both condemning and overwhelming. When I asked the financial secretary about the giving records, I learned that even after a couple of years in the church, after months of intense training in core disciplines of faith, many of them remained disqualified from leadership because of their pitiful giving practices.

There is an enormous amount of research about American church life that demonstrates the old 80/20 rule-of-thumb is gone. You know—80% percent of the money and service is given and demonstrated by 20% of the people. The new stat is 90/10 and the 10% is turning gray or coloring their gray. Look around your own congregation. What happens when the 70-somethings are gone?

What happens when the largest transfer of wealth occurs? What happens when today's octogenarians leave their estates to their baby boomer children? Unless there is careful estate planning by the faithful, we already see evidences by early boomers that they are more inclined to squander their inheritance on themselves. Casino operators are already salivating. Internet gambling (gaming) syndicates are heavily lobbying Washington and your local state capital to reduce restraints and regulations. Entertainment industry is geared up and ready to go to sell the latest and greatest experience, trip, condo or toy.

Lest one think that Western Civilization is on a slippery slope and there is no turning back, let me throw out a lifeline. Great movements of God are often preceded by the indulgence of people in the things that gratify the flesh. Then, when people find themselves trapped and under the oppression of tyrants and trouble, they call out to the Lord. It is part of the nature of cultures to find other things to occupy the hearts and minds of people until they are in desperate straits with no solutions other than to turn to God.

Are we desperate enough to turn to God in the realm of finances? The Christian community today is giving less of a percentage of their incomes to the cause of Christ than people did during the Great Depression. Those were the days when it was fairly common for parents to do without food so that their children could eat. That was a day when self-discipline, frugality, ingenuity and industry sowed the seed for the greatest economic power in human history.

That was also the time Southern Baptists learned the power of cooperative giving to reach the vast lostness of this nation and the world. It was during these days of dark economic duress that Southern Baptists began to work toward a common cooperative giving methodology that has become the envy of evangelical missions. As a result, not only do we have fully supported international missionaries and domestic strategies to reach the most unreached locations in this nation and the world, but we are also training at our six seminaries the next generation of leaders with the tools for effective ministry and missions.

But all of that can be lost in one generation. All it takes is one generation that thinks the Acts 1:8 mandate is optional for Christians. All it takes is one generation to believe they can independently do their own missions thing more effectively and efficiently than the army of cooperating churches. All it takes is a generation that ignores the principles of God's Word about discipline, giving and receiving. All it takes is one generation saying that Jesus is Lord but bowing to the god of consumerism in practice.

In the context of preaching about Lordship in the sphere of giving, what must happen so the pulpit and the pew are walking together in faithfulness before God?

There must be a renewed emphasis on the realities of the Word. When we focus on the truth of the Word and people capture the reality of the Word of God in their everyday living, the world changes; the church changes. When was the last time the preacher and the pew did a spiritual audit of their personal behaviors in light of the Word of God? The brutal, the radical question of life has nothing to do with how many, how much or how did you? It has to do with what is the sum total of your life as it is reflected by the principles of the Word of God? Make the Word of God your standard for decision making.

There must be the release of the prophet of God. If we are not careful, our churches can silence the prophet and relegate his message to irrelevancy for the sake of personal indulgence. Too many churches have harnessed the pastor/prophet. What pastor hasn't heard the talk? "All he does is preach about money." "There he goes again, money, money, money." "Preacher, we deacons think you have preached too much about money."

Churches must renew the teaching of old that declares the man of God they call their pastor is not a hireling. He is the called-out one who consistently has a message from the Lord for the people and leads the church to fulfill its mission. The churches that figure that out and release their personal expectations of what a pastor is supposed to be and do, have the greatest opportunity to achieve God's pleasure.

There must be faithful men in the pulpit. How many pastors have not shown themselves trustworthy and faithful? When the man doesn't exercise good judgment with his time, his words, his study, his relationships, his computer, his eyes and his finances, the people of God begin to discredit his message and justifiably so. We must be found faithful to the end.

There must be men of character in the pew. Part of the beauty of the New Testament church is the concept of holding one another accountable with the things of God. The man of God must equip the people of God in the concepts of devotion. What does that look like? Character, integrity, generosity…the attributes of God.

These sermons are desperately needed in today's American evangelical church. We need to recapture the passion and the practice of these preachers of the Word. Learn from them and trust the Lord with your finances.

John L. Yeats
Director of Communications,
Louisiana Baptist Convention

1

The Chest of Joash
2 CHRONICLES 24:1-14 (KJV)
Jerry Vines
President of 1977 Pastors' Conference

There are a number of subjects that are very sensitive for a preacher to address. I'm going to talk today on probably one of the most sensitive of them all.

Sex is a very sensitive subject to address. But I have done that. For 14 Sunday mornings I brought a series of messages entitled, "Sex according to God," from the Song of Solomon. We had the biggest crowd we have ever had in this building.

But that's not the most sensitive subject. Then sometimes political topics are very sensitive, especially every four years when it gets around election time. I think the ugliest letter I ever received, and I've received some doosies, was after I preached right before the election this year, a message entitled, "The Eyes of Jesus Are Upon You." I said that when you go into the ballot box and you get ready to vote, the eyes of Jesus are upon you. I don't know why that upset them so badly. I didn't know how they were going to vote, but they got very upset about that. Politics can be a very sensitive subject.

I'm going to talk this morning about what I think is the most sensitive subject for a preacher to address and that's the subject of giving.

Somebody gave me a cartoon from Dennis the Menace. It's the picture of a preacher, and a man and his wife and a little boy. The little boy is saying to his dad, "If we give him his money now, will he let us go home early?"

I heard about a preacher who was looking for a different way to get the people to give. They had a big building program going on and needed to raise a lot of money. He hit on the idea of wiring up some of the pews in the building. When he made his appeal, he would just flip the switch of that particular pew.

He said, "We need some people in the church to give $500 to this building program." He pulled the switch and 50 people stood involuntarily. That got him excited. He said, "We need some people in this church who will give $1,000 to this building program." He flipped the switch and 15 people stood involuntarily. By then he was really worked up. He decided that he would pull the main switch. He said, "We need some folks in this church who will give $10,000 to this project." He pulled the switch and 40 deacons were electrocuted.

This is a sensitive subject but it is a very important subject because everything you see in this building is made possible because of the giving of the congregation here at First Baptist Church in Jacksonville.

The Bible is just filled with passages that have to do with the subject of giving. I have tried in the years that I have been your pastor to give you the whole counsel of God. If the Lord will help me finish up the series in the book of Deuteronomy, I will have preached a series of messages on every book in the Bible. I have dealt with every conceivable subject and topic and truth I have known to give to you.

But I don't think there is anything I can do for you or say to you that will be any more helpful or that will be any more needed in your life than the subject of what God has to say about the matter of giving.

I'm going to talk to you about the unique way our church has gone about raising the money to do the things that we want to do. I'm going to share with you, on the basis of the Scripture. I have read to you this morning, how we have gone about it and the reason we have done it the way we have done it. I'm going to talk to you about the significance of what we do biblically. I'm going to talk to you about how significant it is for our church historically, and then I'm going to talk to you about how it impacts your life personally.

It is an Old Testament passage of Scripture. It is a familiar account to many of you who have been members of our church for a long time. But others of you who recently joined our church, or some of you who are new Christians and are just beginning to read your Bible, this may be a brand new passage of Scripture for you.

It is the account of the young king, Joash, who was used by God to develop a method to finance the work of the Lord that needed to be done.

The King's Thoughtful Preparation

First of all, in the opening verses, I want you to think about what I am going to call, "The King's Thoughtful Preparation."

We have an unusual situation here. Here is a boy who became king at the age of 7. He was guided by the priest in that day. When someone became king at a very early age, a priest would guide him until the age of maturity. Here is an example of a young man who was used by the Lord.

I want to say to all of our young people that God can use you even though you are young. Some of the best Christians we have in our church are young people. Some of the most committed members of our church and some of the finest soul winners are young people. Don't think that because you are young you are out of the loop. God can use you.

He was young. He was 7 when he started. The Bible says in verse 2 that young Joash did what was right in the sight of the Lord.

That's a good way to start. Do what is right in the sight of the Lord. It's not always easy to do right. It's not always the popular thing to do right.

William Penn said, "Right is right even if everybody is against it. Wrong is wrong even if everybody is for it."

Bob Jones, Sr., used to say, "Do right if the stars fall." It is always right to do right.

I want to talk to you about doing the right thing. "He did what was right."

Notice the purpose that motivates this young king, Joash. It says in verse 4, "*That Joash was minded to repair the house of the Lord.*" In other words, Joash saw the condition of the house of the Lord and he had a heart; he was minded to repair; to mend the house of the Lord.

The house of the Lord in those days was a temple. In the Old Testament, the children of Israel started off with a tabernacle, which was a portable building. Then when they moved into Jerusalem, they built a permanent building, the Temple. But it was getting old. It was a magnificent building, but buildings do get old.

Evidently, Joash had gone through the building on an inspection tour. He saw that the roof was leaking and there was water coming inside the house of the Lord. Some of the boards were coming unglued from the walls. Some of the curtains were getting faded and worn. There was paint peeling off of the walls. There were cobwebs in the corner. The young king said, "We can't have this. This is the house of the Lord. We can't let God's house go down like this."

Of course, we know that everything in our world has a tendency to go down. It is one of the laws of thermodynamics that everything is winding down. By the way, that is one of the laws which disprove evolution. Evolution says that everything is going up. It's getting better and better. But we know the truth of the matter is that there is a tendency for everything to go down.

That brand-new car of yours that you bought four years ago has gone down a little bit now. It's getting a little bit worn. Things tend to go down.

I think about our buildings here. We have a long history of building. We have bought property and we have constructed a number of buildings. Can you believe that this building we are in is 13 years old? It's amazing, isn't it? Buildings wear out. Carpet gets a little bit worn.

We have some buildings we bought a number of years ago. There's a story in every one of these buildings. Our administration building was the old Gulf Life building. It was a magnificent building. My study has wood on the walls. But the plumbing gets old in buildings like that. We have a lot of buildings that need to be repaired. They need to be mended. It is very expensive to do that. We have on the board here a number of repair and renovation projects.

I want you to notice that love for the Lord and love for the house of the Lord go together. You can tell a great deal about how people feel about the Lord by the condition of the buildings where they go to worship Him.

When I walk in a building and I see a run down, shabby, unkempt building, it tells me something about what those people think about God. Our buildings make a statement. I believe that the most magnificent, the best kept, the most glorious buildings in a city should be the buildings where the people of God worship the Lord. I believe that with all of my heart.

CHAPTER ONE

I remember a number of years ago when I was living in Georgia, there was a church building a million dollar facility. That sounds like peanuts to us now, but in those days a million dollars was a lot of money. At the same time, they were constructing the football stadium where the Falcons play.

I can recall all of the letters that came to the editor of the Atlanta newspaper belittling and criticizing and throwing off on the church for spending a million dollars to build a building. As I recall they spent 120 million dollars to build a football stadium where 22 men in need of rest are watched by 50,000 people in need of exercise, and nobody had a word to say.

Do you think that maybe in this country we have our sense of values out of whack? We are living in a country where they will pay a guy 5 million dollars to catch a football, and yet we have missionaries sitting in this service right here this morning who have a struggle to get by and barely meet their needs. Is there something a little bit out of whack with our values in America? The love for the Lord and the love for the house of the Lord go together. You can't separate them.

Jesus loved the church, the Bible says, and gave Himself for it. I love my church. If you should cut me, my blood would flow First Baptist Church of Jacksonville. I love my church.

I've never understood people who criticize their church. Bailey Smith used to talk about a guy in a church. The pastor said to him, "Bro. Jones, would you please stand and lead us in a word of criticism?"

If I couldn't find anything I liked about the church I was attending, I would join a church where I could find something I liked. I love my church. We're not a perfect church, but I love my church. This is my church. "For her my tears shall fall. To her my prayers ascend. To her my hopes and fears be given until hopes and fears shall end." This is my church. You need to love your church.

Joash loved the house of the Lord. God put it in his mind and in his heart to repair, to renovate the house of the Lord.

In verse 5 Joash calls the people together and he says, "*Gather of all Israel's money to repair the house of your God from year to year, and hasten the matter.*" Do it now. Let's get busy right now.

The time to do something for the Lord is when the Lord lays it on your heart to do it. Some of you have been planning for years to do something big for God. When are you going to do it? You better do it now.

In the book of Ephesians, chapter 5, verse 16, it says, "*Redeeming the time, because the days are evil.*"

Our country is rapidly becoming an anti-Christian culture. The freedoms you and I enjoy and the opportunities you and I have to be a witness for the Lord Jesus Christ are in jeopardy unless God sends America a revival of faith in Jesus Christ.

It's getting politically incorrect to even talk about sin. Did you know it is entirely possible that the day will come when a preacher gets up and calls something sin that he could be accused of a hate crime? It's happening in Canada right now.

It says at the end of verse 5, "*Howbeit, the Levites hastened it not.*" One paraphrase says, "*They dragged their feet and did nothing about it.*"

We don't have that luxury now. It's time for us to do something for God right now. It's time for us to witness for Jesus Christ right now. It's time for us to win as many people to faith in the Lord as we can right now. There is never a good time. Anytime you talk about doing something for God there are always some reasons why you can't.

When you talk about the matter of giving, there are always reasons why you can't. The economy is not good. The price of gas is going out the roof. We don't know about the stock market. For most of us the stock market is not a big problem. Some people are into the stock market. Some people are into the bond market. Most of us are into the flea market, so it's not a big deal.

I had my 68th birthday Thursday. I saw a lady gasp when I said that. She couldn't believe I was 68, but I am. Bruce Whorton sent me this about the prices in 1937. A gallon of milk was fifty cents. A loaf of bread was nine cents. A new automobile was $675 dollars. A gallon of gas was twelve cents. When I moved here 23 years ago, I filled up my car in Rome, Georgia, to drive down here. I paid twenty four cents for a gallon of gas. A new home was $6,622. The average annual income was $1,227.

There is never a good time. There is always a reason why you can't give. There is always a reason why you can't do the things that God wants you to do.

But here is a man who had a purpose in his heart. Here is a man who called upon the people of God to do something big for God. They didn't do it. They delayed. What he had suggested, now he commands.

You will notice in verse 8 that it says, "And at the king's commandment." In other words, the king stepped in and he took the bull by the horns and he said, "We are going to do something about this situation."

That's what a pastor does. There are times that a pastor has to step in and take the bull by the horns.

That's what the king is doing here. He says, "We are going to do according to the king's command." He had a plan to get it done. Notice what he did. The Bible says in verse 8, "*And at the king's commandment they made a chest, and set it outside at the gate of the house of the Lord.*"

There is a parallel account in 1 Kings, chapter 12, that tells us a little bit more about that chest. We are told in verse 9 that they took a chest and bore a hole in the lid of it and set it before the altar. In other words, they took that chest and put it by the altar in the Temple.

That's an interesting juxtaposition there. As you know in the Old Testament those sacrifices that were put on that altar were fulfilled in the sacrifice of Jesus on the cross. Every time you read about a sacrifice in the Old Testament, just in your mind say, "All that was fulfilled when Jesus died on the cross."

In front of you is a chest that has been constructed in order for the people to give. It is put alongside an altar which depicts the sacrifice of Jesus Christ on the cross.

The greatest motivation for giving is the sacrifice that Jesus made when He died for our sins on the cross of Calvary. If Jesus gave His all on the cross, that becomes a motivation for us to be a giver to the Lord in return.

They built this chest. That's why we have this replica here. This is not the chest of Joash. This is a replica of the chest of Joash.

This chest has been in the life of our church for 65 years. On October 9 you will find other replicas of the chest of Joash all over this building.

Dr. Homer Lindsay, Sr., came here in 1940 and the church was bankrupt. He started a program to get the church out of debt. He began to preach on tithing. His brother built the replica of the chest of Joash for him. He put that in front of the congregation over in the old Hobson building.

We have three auditoriums in our church. That is unheard of. I don't know if I know a church anywhere that has three auditoriums. We have the Hobson auditorium. We have the Ruth Lindsay auditorium and we have this main auditorium.

He put this chest in the Hobson. When he did, everything broke lose. Talk about upsetting people. He was going to ask the people to come down and put their commitment to tithe to the Lord in the chest. Of course, the seven last words of a dead church came up, "We never did it this way before." He had opposition. But any of you who knew Dr. Lindsay, Sr., have to know that opposition never did hinder him in any way. He just kept on doing it and kept on doing it. It got the church out of debt and that's how the church began to make its commitment to stay debt free, and we have been doing that continually for 65 years.

Right here in this chest and in the other replicas, every commitment we have made to build every building we have built around here, to do every project we are planning to do, has all been committed right here.

Here's what will happen on "Chest of Joash" Sunday. There will be three things you will be asked to do. Number one, you will be asked to make a commitment to the budget of our church and a commitment to tithe. Number two, you will be asked to make a commitment to the building fund of our church. Number three, you will be asked to make a special offering to finish out the television ministry. We are installing brand new television equipment.

The choice was very simple on this. The equipment you see around here is anywhere from 11 to 14 years old. We have literally searched around the world to find replacement parts for this equipment, and now we are at the point that the decision was made to either stay on television or go off of television.

Every week we get testimonies about people who are saved watching television. A lady and her daughter came last Sunday to the reception and told me that they were saved watching us on television. They joined the church last Sunday night and will probably be baptized tonight. It was all because of our television ministry.

That's a no brainer. We are going to stay on television. But if we do, then we can't buy that equipment anymore which cost 2.8 million dollars 14 years ago. We had to go to new technology, which is going to cost us over 3 million dollars. We don't know exactly what it will be. We are almost there. But what we need is a good, special offering and finish that out so we can finish the project and get the projection IMags bigger. Everything we have done, we have done it through the commitment of this chest of Joash.

That's how the king was going to do the work and that's how we are going to do the work here.

The People's Faithful Demonstration

The day came and the Bible says in verse 9 that they made a proclamation and in verse 10 it says that all the people came and brought and cast into the chest.

Did you notice that not a single name is used? It just says the people. Every time I read that I think about the unnamed heroes in the fellowship of the First Baptist Church of Jacksonville. You are here and faithful in your attendance. You are faithful in your giving. You are faithful to serve and work here. You are not doing it to get your name mentioned. You are not doing it in order to get attention. But you do it because you love Jesus and you love lost people and you want our church to be a soul winning station for the Lord.

Here come the people. They are giving obediently. You will notice that it was according to the collection that Moses laid upon Israel. What was that? Malachi 3, verse 10, is what it was all about. *"Bring all the tithes into the storehouse, that there may be meat in mine house, and prove me now herewith, saith the Lord of hosts."*

We believe the starting point is to give God ten percent of your income. If you make a hundred dollars, then you give God ten dollars. Then we believe in giving offerings over and above. You have always responded.

If you are looking for a reason not to give, you will always find it. I heard about a farmer and his friend who were talking together. The friend said to the farmer, "If you had a thousand hogs, would you give me half of them?" He said, "Bubba, I'd give you half of them."

Then the friend said, "If you had five hundred hogs, would you give me half of them?" He said, "I'd give you half of my hogs."

The friend said to the farmer, "If you had two hogs would you give me one of them?" The farmer said, "You know that isn't fair. You know I've got two hogs."

If you don't want to give, you can always find a reason not to give. There is always a way to wiggle around it.

I heard about an old man who was a miser. Every dime he made, he saved. His poor old wife never had anything. He wouldn't spend anything on her. He just loved that money.

He finally said to her, "Listen, when I die, I want every dime I've got put in the grave with me." He got out the Bible and made her put her hand on the Bible that when he died every dime of money he had would go in the grave with him.

The man died. At the funeral, while wiping away tears, she had a box. She was sitting at the graveside and a friend of hers was there with her. She said, "What's that box for?" She said, "My husband made me promise that when he died I would put every dime he had in the grave with him." Her friend looked at her and said, "You are not going to do that, are you?" She said, "I made a promise. I'm a Christian and I'm going to keep my promise."

When the time came she went to the grave with that box and her friend said, "I can't believe you are actually going to do that." She said, "Yes, I'm a Christian but I'm no fool. I wrote him a check."

When you really don't want to do something, you will find a way out. You will find something you don't like. You will find something to criticize. You will find some reason not to give.

But the people gave obediently. They gave joyfully. The Bible says that they rejoiced.

The Bible says in 2 Kings 12 that all the money that comes into any man's heart, bring it into the house of the Lord. The word there means to ascend as a king. It's saying to let giving ascend as a king in your heart.

Do it voluntarily. We don't come to your house, sit down and try to talk you into giving.

I heard about a member who was all worked up and wanted to do something for the Lord. He just kept pestering his pastor and he said, "I want to do something, pastor."

So finally the preacher said, "Here's a list of names of people who haven't attended and haven't given in a long time. Write all those people a letter and encourage them to renew their attendance and renew their giving."

About a week later he got a letter from one of the members. It said, "Dear pastor, I realize that I have not been as active as I should have been and I have not been attending the services regularly. Furthermore, I have not been faithful financially to the work of the church. I am enclosing a check for $5,000 and I assure you that I will be at all the services from now on."

Then at the bottom of the page there was a P.S. "Dear pastor, would you please tell your secretary that there is only one "t" in dirty and no "c" in skunk." We don't do it that way around here.

They gave voluntarily. They gave cheerfully. They gave plentifully.

The Bible says in verse 11 that they gave much money.

The last part of verse 11 says, "*And gathered money in abundance.*" They gave generously. They gave sacrificially.

The Temple's Beautiful Renovation

The last thought is the Temple's beautiful renovation. They took the money and they put it in the hands of the people to do the work.

We have a finance committee. They are as diligent and committed as any group I have ever known. On that committee we have bankers and lawyers and financial planners. We have managers and executives and retired and just ordinary working men. We have all kinds.

It takes seven people to approve any check that is signed at First Baptist Church of Jacksonville, Florida. You can have absolute confidence in the integrity of how your money is cared for.

They put it in the hands of the workers. We put it in the hands of our music staff. We put it in the hands of our educational people and they develop the programs to help us reach people. We put it in the hands of our young people. We put it in the hands of missionaries so they can go forward winning people to faith in Christ.

The Temple was beautifully renovated. That's what giving is all about. Let me encourage you to get involved in being a giver and not a taker.

2

When God's Money Hurts Yours
Haggai 1-2 (KJV)
Bailey E. Smith
President of 1978 Pastors' Conference

When I was pastor of the First Baptist Church of Hobbs, New Mexico, I was having lunch with one of our members when he started a verbal diatribe against people on welfare. He said, "These people on welfare are just leeches. They're lazy bums. You work and I work and we pay our taxes and these no-goods are living on what we pay the government because they don't pay any taxes. They get commodities, food stamps etc., etc.… " So, I went back to the church and checked his giving record. He had given less than $20.00 for the seven months of the year.

I called him and asked him to have lunch the following day. He agreed and we met at Ross Richards Steak House. We both had far too much for lunch – rib-eye steak, baked potato and a side of pinto beans. I would love to be there now. While eating his butter and sour cream laden baked potato, I said, "Jack, I checked your giving record at the church." It was the first time I had ever seen a man swallow a baked potato whole. Then I said, "When are you going to get off church member welfare?" He got the point.

There are people in our pews that are disgusted by the people in our country living off the giving of others. However, they are just as guilty in the church. They are enjoying somebody else's preaching, somebody else's music, somebody else's carpet and somebody else's air-condition because they don't give enough to have any of that. Simply, they don't tithe. They are enjoying what the tithers and givers pay for. They are on church member welfare.

What the non-tithers don't understand is that they will not have more money, they will have less. Why? Because when you mix God's money that you have kept and then place it next to yours in your wallet, it diseases your money. Our text will make this crystal clear but I want us to look at the broader story. I will finish with a convincing argument that to keep God's money (the tithe) diseases and diminishes the 90% you kept.

Our reading is from the time of 520 B.C., when Israel, after captivity, was told to rebuild the temple in Jerusalem and the people were sternly encouraged to do so by Haggai and Zachariah. Haggai is letting them know God's great displeasure with their lack of giving and the Lord was punishing them severely for that very reason.

Note Israel's three mistakes but their eventual blessings are all described in the book of Haggai.

Their Misplaced Priorities (v. 1:4)

"Is it time for you, O ye, to dwell in your cieled houses, and this house lie in waste?" Then the Lord says (v.1:6c) *"...and he that earneth wages puts it into a bag with holes."* Haggai, the prophet, is responding to the people who said it was not time to build the temple because they didn't want to pay the price. So he responds by telling them (v.5) "Consider your ways!" He is letting them know they have money for themselves, but not for the Lord.

Oh my! Does that misplaced sense of priorities exist today? When I was a pastor, I was standing at the check-out counter right behind one of my non-tithers. He had bought things like a manual lawn edger (This was 1980), fertilizer, weed killer and hedge trimmer – everything imaginable for his yard – over $600.00. I do remember how his yard and landscaping looked - immaculate. I believe some people think when they die they are going to their yard. That would be paradise enough for them.

As I drove away from that store, I remembered the times when that man told me he thought tithing was too much and he couldn't afford it. No, he just loved his house more than he loved God's house. It really was not that he believed tithing was restricted to the Old Testament, but rather he was trying to use the Bible to rationalize his stinginess – his misplaced priorities.

Tithing was before the law, during the law and after the law. Any Christian under grace who gives less than an Israelite under the law is a disgrace to grace.

Notice secondly their:

Misjudged Purpose (v. 1:8c)

Why is the Lord telling them to give? Here it is in verse 8, "…*and I will take pleasure in it and I will be glorified*…" Should that not be the desire of every Christian to please and glorify the Lord? If only every child of our holy God believed that, tithing would never be an issue. It would be an eager joy.

God in His Word always had something special for Himself. In the Garden of Eden, it was a tree. In the days of the week it is the Sabbath, our Sunday. In terms of money, it is the dime out of every dollar, 10%, the tithe. It is God's whether you give it or not. Our purpose is to please and glorify the Lord. So when we give; churches are built; people who labor in the Christian ministry daily are supported; missionaries are sent across the earth; the message of Christ and eternal life can be preached by radio and television. The hungry can be fed and all of this pleases the Lord. Let's not forget our purpose.

Paul said in Philippians, "*For me to live is Christ and to die is gain.*" Life is Christ. That's it.

Why do we get up every morning? Christ. Why do we rear children? We do it to send out more Christian warriors into the world. Why do we make money? For the purpose of supporting the fulfillment of Christ's Great Commission in Matthew 28:19-20. If every Christian would tithe to their church, this evil world could be dramatically changed in a matter of months. No, that is not overstated. Look at the great good that has been done by the pitiful few who do tithe.

Thirdly, I want you to see from one of the most profound analogies in the Bible their:

Malignant Possessions (v. 2:11-14)

We have already seen they were putting money into bags where it was falling right back out. The Lord also said in 1:6, "*Ye have sown much and bring in little, ye eat but have not enough, ye drink but are not filled with drink…*"

But why? Haggai explains in profound illustration beginning in verse 11. "*Thus saith the Lord of hosts; 'Ask now the priest concerning the law, saying, If one bear holy flesh in the skirt of his garment, and with his skirt do touch bread, or pottage, or wine, or oil, or any meat, shall it be holy?' And the priests answered and said, 'No.' Then said Haggai, 'If one that is unclean by a dead body touch any of these, shall it be unclean?' The priests answered and said, 'It shall be unclean.' Then answered Haggai, and said, 'So is this people, and so is this nation before me, saith the Lord; and so is every work of their hands; and that which they offer there is unclean.'*"

Here is what he is saying in today's understanding. Can Billy Graham touch a sinner and make him clean? No. Could a man with tuberculosis infect Billy Graham? Yes. Holiness cannot be simply given to another but disease can be. Why does the Lord say in 2:14b what the people are giving is "unclean"? It is not enough. It is inadequate. It is not what the Lord requires. It is ineffectual.

What is the result? They are putting diseased money up against the money they have and it is hurting their own funds. It does not buy what it should. It is diminished because they are putting back into their wallets stolen money – money stolen from a holy and righteous God.

God's money will hurt your money when you keep His and mix it in with yours. Wow! No wonder so many are having financial problems. You say, "Well, money is tight." NO, church members are tight. You need to urgently get rid of all of God's money you have hoarded and you will see how healthy your money becomes when God blesses it as only He can.

A dear friend of mine was a wealthy businessman. He knew he had not tithed for years. He had his accountant go back twenty years and discover how much he would have given had he tithed. The next Sunday he wrote a check to his Missouri church for over $700,000. He really prospered then because God's money was no longer defiling his. Learn that lesson.

Last of all, on a note of God's goodness to an obedient people, see their:

Magnificent Promise

In Haggai 2:19b, very simply God says, "…*from this day will I bless you.*" The Lord describes later this promised blessing in more encouraging detail. Do we not all who tithe have the same promise in Malachi 3:10b "…*I will open you the windows of heaven and pour you out a blessing that there shall not be room enough to receive it.*"

You can believe you are smarter than God and try to spend His money in your own way or you can be obedient and watch the windows of heaven cascade blessings to you that no amount of your wisdom could ever provide.

Henry Ward Beecher said, "There never was a person who did anything worth doing, who did not receive more than he gave." That's good, but guess what? God said it first.

A friend of mine was brought up on a farm where he had to work very hard. One hot day his dad said, "Son, I've got to take the old truck into town to get some supplies." He said, "Dad, I want to go with you." The dad said, "No, son, I've driven a stake in the field and when I get home I want to see that you have ploughed from the house to the stake." The boy confessed he deeply resented his dad leaving him there to plough. As he worked he started thinking of all his father had done for him and his family – the labor in the field, odd jobs late into the night to provide for all of the needs of the family. His attitude changed from anger to appreciation.

That evening when the father returned he noticed the son had ploughed not only from the house to the stake, but from the stake to the barn. The father said, "Terry, I told you to plough from the house to the stake, but you ploughed all the way to the barn. Can you tell me why?" He said, "When you left me to work I was not happy, but as I worked I realized how hard you had worked for us and my heart changed. So, Dad, I ploughed from the house to the stake because you made me, but I ploughed from the stake out to the barn because I love you."

Sometimes, we should do some things just because we love the Lord. Surely, tithing is the minimal way to express our love for the One who kept us out of Hell. No price could be put on that. So joyfully give for gratitude and yes, blessing.

3

Setting the Stewardship Standard
Proverbs 3:9-10 (NKJV™)
O.S. Hawkins
President of 1985 Pastors' Conference

There are many pastors and churches that avoid the subject of stewardship like a plague. In fact, many modern church gurus are telling pastors across the country not to talk about money or stewardship. I find that to be very strange since our Lord spoke of it in one-third of His parables. In the churches I was privileged to pastor, we made no apologies in challenging one another in the realm of stewardship for it was a great part of our own spiritual development and growth.

Money consumes us in our current culture. Our churches are full of financial planners, bankers, stockbrokers, money managers, venture capitalists, CPAs, lawyers, and all kinds of men and women who are constantly giving financial counsel. How would you like the free counsel of a man recognized the world over as one of the richest, most successful, and wisest men who ever lived? This particular man "wrote the book" on international commerce. In fact, of him it was said, "*God gave (him) wisdom and exceedingly great understanding, and largeness of heart like the sand on the seashore. Thus (his) wisdom excelled the wisdom of all the men of the East and all the wisdom of Egypt. For he was wiser than all men – than Ethan the Ezrahite, and Heman, Chalcol, and Darda, the sons of Mahol; and his fame was in all the surrounding nations. He spoke three thousand proverbs, and his songs were one thousand and five*" (1 Kings 4:29-32). His name? Solomon. Listen to his counsel on money management. "*Honor the Lord with your possessions, and with the firstfruits of all your increase; so your barns will be filled with plenty, and your vats will overflow with new wine"* (Prov. 3:9-10).

As far-fetched as it might seem, our finances generally mark the position of our own spiritual pilgrimage. We are no farther along in our walk with the Lord than the point in which we learn to trust Him with the tithe.

There are a lot of questions regarding stewardship. How can we afford to return one-tenth of our income back to God? How much should we give? There are four questions every believer should ask about stewardship: (1) What is the purpose of my stewardship? (2) What is the product of my stewardship? (3) What is the priority of my stewardship? (4) What is the promise of my stewardship?

What Is The Purpose Of My Stewardship?

"Honor the Lord…" Proverbs 3:9-10

What is the purpose when we attend a worship service and the offering plate is passed and we place our gift in it? Note the first three words of our text – "Honor the Lord." This should be our single most important goal in life - to honor God. It is always a good thing to check our motivation, our purpose regarding the issues of life. Honoring God should be our primary motive in everything we do, whether in our marriage, our social life, our business, or whatever.

What is the purpose of our stewardship? Some are motivated by guilt. That is, they give because they think they ought to. Others are grudge givers. That is, they give because they think they have to. The New Testament teaches us to be grace givers – we give out of a heart of gratitude and love because we want to!

The Hebrew word that we translate into our English word "honor" is very enlightening at this point. What does it mean when we are exhorted to "honor God?" Often this word is used to describe the concept of being weighted down. For example, a king is weighted down with all the accessories of royalty the crown, the robe, the train, the scepter and the medallion. When we honor God it means that we weigh Him down. Crown Him Lord!

It is closely akin to what young people used to say, "That's heavy!" This being translated means, "That is incomprehensible, awesome, powerful." To say that we honor God means that we give Him His rightful place in our lives. He is Lord!

What is the purpose of our stewardship? Is it some lucky rabbit's foot? Is it that I give so that I might get, as some teach? Is it some legalistic Old Testament discipline that keeps me bound to the law? Our purpose in stewardship has to do with honoring God by exhibiting trust in Him.

We are nothing more than stewards passing through this world. Fifty years from now everything you own will be in someone else's name. Fifty years ago what is in your name today was in someone else's; your land, your home, your assets. When you entered this world, you entered it naked without a dime, and you will leave it the same way. In reality, we do not own a thing. We are simply stewards. Therefore, it is imperative that we honor God with our possessions. This is our purpose in stewardship. God makes an incredible statement in 1 Samuel 2:30 when He says, "Those who honor Me I will honor." What is the purpose of our stewardship? It is to honor God!

What Is The Product Of My Stewardship?

"…*with your possessions…*" Proverbs 3:9-10

We are to honor God. With what? Our possessions, our money, our wealth. Note the product of our stewardship is not just our time. It is not simply our talents. This is not what Solomon is saying. It is our treasure that is specifically addressed here.

Some of us live as if our lives were a hotel corridor with room after room. As God walks down the hall, He sees the family room with the door open for Him to come in. He sees our social room, our work room, our exercise room, our activity room, our hobby room, and they are all open to Him. But in many lives when it comes to the room where we have our possessions, our money, He sees a "Do Not Disturb" sign on that door.

What is the one thing that is prone to dominate and dictate our lives? Money! In fact, God says in 1 Timothy 6: 10 that, "*The love of money is a root of all kinds of evil.*" We get trapped by government policies and our own lifestyles into thinking that money is the answer to every problem. How many times have we asked someone how they were doing, only to have heard the reply that everything was okay and they had no problems that money would not solve! Thus, the Lord indicates an area of our lives which tells us more about our spiritual condition than any other. He says it is our possessions, and hence Solomon says, "*Honor God with your possessions.*"

It is good to have things that money can buy. However, there is something better. It is to have what money cannot buy. We have recently had another first in our family. Our oldest daughter, Wendy, is now wearing a wedding ring. As I write these words I am thinking back to the ring I gave her mom. It is now in a stickpin. I was a student in 1970 and could only afford a small ring. I remember the salesman making a special deal on the particular ring I purchased because if you look closely enough you will see a big carbon spot in the middle of it. I would be embarrassed for her to know how little I paid for it. However, that ring symbolized a tremendous amount of love as well as the confidence that God had brought us together.

At about the same time a college friend gave his fiancée one of the biggest, most beautiful diamond rings I have ever seen, worth thousands of dollars. The tragedy is that their marriage did not last a year. Money can buy a lot of things. It can buy million dollar houses, but all the money in the world cannot transform a house into a home. What is really important is not what money can buy, but what it cannot buy.

While some of us desire to honor God with our lives we never think of honoring Him with our possessions. How do we do this? There are three ways in which we honor God with our possessions.

First, we honor God with how we *get* it. Some people get wealth in ways that are dishonoring to God.

We also can honor or dishonor God by the way we *guard* it. The Lord Jesus said in Matthew 6:19, "*Do not lay up for yourselves treasures on earth.*" Many guard their wealth. Some even make arrangements to keep it hoarded and guarded even after they are gone. It is no accident that our last will is called our Last Will and Testament, or Testimony. It is the last opportunity we have to give our testimony to the world of what was really important to us. One day someone will read it and tell what really held your heart because Jesus said, "*Where your treasure is, there your heart will be also*" (Matt. 6:21).

James spoke of a man who "hoarded" his wealth (James 5:3). Some people get their stock portfolios or checking and savings statements each month. No matter how much we have, we wish it were just a little bit more. When we begin to love money, it ceases to bless us and begins to curse us. No wonder Solomon said, "*Honor the Lord with your possessions.*"

God is as concerned with how we guard our wealth as He is with how we get it. Susie and I do not have much of an estate after one-quarter century of marriage. We have invested in the bank of heaven. Much of the savings of our first twenty years of marriage is in the auditorium in Fort Lauderdale, Florida, where hundreds of people came to know Christ every year and from where dozens of missionaries have been sent.

Our daughters know they are not going to get much from us. I intend to leave them something far more important than a pile of money to hoard or to guard or even to throw away. We have sought to teach them the importance of laying up treasures in heaven. Why? Because our heart always follows our treasure (Matt. 6:21). If we wait until we feel like giving, we will never do it. The natural man wants to guard it. Thus Solomon gives us wise counsel when he says we are to "Honor God with our possessions."

We honor God by not only how we get and guard our money, but also with how we *give* it. We are stewards of God's blessing. How we give is vitally important. The Lord Jesus still sits over the treasuries to see how His people give. One day I will stand before this great God. He is not going to say to me, "Let me see your Bible." Quite frankly there is not a page in my Bible that is not marked and filled with notations. He is not going to look at me and ask, "Is your Bible all marked?" He is not going to say, "Let me see your sermon notebook. Are there any notes there?" I don't believe He is even going to ask for my prayer journal. Some of us may be shocked. I think He might say, "Let me see your checkbook, I want to look at your cancelled checks." Why? Because how we use what He gives us tells us where our heart is. He said, "*Where your treasure is, there your heart will be also*" (Matt. 6:21).

This is the purpose and product of our stewardship. The way we handle our possessions is so much a reflection of what is on the inside of us that our Lord Jesus Christ addressed it in one out of three of His recorded sermons and His parables.

What Is The Priority Of My Stewardship?
"*…with the firstfruits of all your increase…*" Proverbs 3:9-10

Note that Solomon is specific with the portion of our possessions with which we are to honor God. He calls it the "firstfruits." The Israelites brought the firstfruits of all their crops to God in order to acknowledge that He was the ultimate owner of the land. God said, *"The land shall not be sold permanently, for the land is Mine; for you are strangers and sojourners with Me"* (Lev. 25:23). God owns the land of Israel today, and by His grace Israel is His tenant. Thus as they brought the firstfruits offerings they were honoring Yahweh. Should we do less?

The first portion of everything we own should be set aside for God's use. The Old and the New Testament both refer to it as the tithe – one-tenth of our income. The New Testament pattern is characterized by freedom. But freedom does not negate the validity of the tithe. The *Believer's Study Bible* note says, "Tithing is only the beginning place of Christian stewardship, not the end. God does not want you to give less than a tithe, but He may want you to give so much more through His enabling grace." For me personally, I have never felt that in this dispensation of grace that I should give less than the Jews gave under the dispensation of the law. Hence, tithing is only the beginning place, the firstfruits.

In his own inimitable way, Dr. W. A. Criswell frames this point with these words, "Four hundred years before the law was given, Father Abraham paid tithes to Melchizedek, priest to the most high God. Tithing was the foundation of supportive worship of the Israelites throughout the dispensation of the law. It was in that era that the Lord Jesus lived and had His being. It was He who said we ought to tithe (Matt. 23:23). In this dispensation in which you and I live, it is the Lord Jesus Christ who receives our tithes even though our human hands take it up in the congregation. Hebrews 7:8 says, *'Here mortal men receive tithes, but there He receives them, of whom it is witnessed that He lives.'*" There is a sense in which every time we receive an offering in church although mortal men are serving as ushers to receive the gifts, it is the Lord Jesus Christ Himself who is receiving them.

What is the priority of our stewardship? We are to honor God. With what? Our wealth. And what part of it? Firstfruits. I well remember the day my pastor, W. Fred Swank, taught me this truth. I was a student at Southwestern Seminary and serving as assistant pastor at Sagamore Hill Baptist Church in Fort Worth, Texas. I was about to be married, and Dr. Swank called me into his office on a particular day. He was known for always being blunt and to the point. He said, "Son, your giving has been a bit sporadic." With those words I knew I was about to learn a lesson. Those of us who were "his boys" never got away with anything! I quickly replied, "Preacher, I am trying to tithe, but I get to the end of the month, and it just seems like there is not enough there." He looked at me and said, "We are to honor God with our possessions, with the firstfruits of all our increase." He continued, "Now, let me see your checkbook." Reluctantly I handed it to him. He asked another question, "What is fruit?" "That which you earn," I quickly replied. He countered, "What does *first* mean?" "First means first, the front of the line!" "Then, when you deposit your check on the first and fifteenth of each month make sure from now on the first check you write is the Lord's tithe, the firstfruits of all your increase," he said.

He went on to explain to me that giving is an act of faith and showed me the meaning of Proverbs 3:5-6 which says we are to, "*Trust the Lord with all of our hearts and lean not unto our own understanding. In all our ways acknowledge Him and He will direct our paths.*" Since that day years ago, I have never deposited a paycheck except that the first check I wrote was "unto the Lord," the firstfruit.

Many years ago, Susie and I discovered the joy of giving way over the tithe every year of our married life. We did it when we had little or nothing. We did it when we were struggling with a young family. And now when we are responsible for college tuition, graduate school tuition, and weddings, we still are blessed by it. It is the priority of our stewardship. I am often asked by people who are contemplating becoming tithers if the tithe is to be given before or after taxes. For me, I never even considered the fact that taxes to a human government should be the firstfruits. To me the issue is plain. Solomon said, "Firstfruits" – of what? "All your increase." That is how we honor God. This is the priority of our stewardship.

If we wait until we think we can afford it and continue to give our firstfruits to ourselves, or to others, or to our own pleasures, it won't happen. An unknown poet framed it best when he or she said,

> *The groom bent with age leaned over his cane*
> *his steps uncertain needed guiding,*
> *while down the church aisle*
> *with a warm toothless smile*
> *the bride in a wheelchair came riding.*
> *Who is this elderly couple thus wed?*
> *We've learned when we quickly explored it,*
> *that this is that rare most conservative pair*
> *who waited till they could afford it!*

Our purpose in life is to honor God. With what? With our possessions. And what part of our possessions? The "firstfruits" of all our possessions. There is one other question of stewardship that all of us should be asking:

What Is The Promise Of My Stewardship?

"…so that your barns may be filled and your vats overflow with new wine." Proverbs 3:9-10

Full and overflowing! This is a far cry from the haunting call of many today – "Not enough." Here we see the John 6 principle in action. The boy gave his little lunch of loaves and fish. Thousands of people were fed and twelve baskets remained. In the words of Solomon, *"Your barns will be filled with plenty and your vats will overflow with new wine."* This is an amazing thought we find in Proverbs 3:10, *"So your barns will be filled with plenty, and your vats will overflow with new wine.*" It is supernatural. I don't know how it works. I just know that after doing it every week for over a quarter of a century it does work. In fact, the words "be filled" in verse 10 are in the imperfect tense. It is an ongoing process. It just continues to be true as I continue to honor God with my possessions, with the firstfruits of all my increase. He just keeps on and on filling my barns.

Have you noticed that when God addresses our stewardship in the Bible, His emphasis is not on our giving, but on our receiving? Malachi says, "'*Bring all the tithes into the storehouse, that there may be food in My house, and try Me now in this,*' says the Lord of hosts, '*If I will not open for you the windows of heaven and pour out for you such a blessing that there will not be room enough to receive it*'" (Mal. 3:10). The emphasis is on our receiving. In Proverbs 3:9-10 once again the emphasis is not on our giving as much as it is on our barns being filled – our receiving. In the New Testament, Jesus said it like this, "*Give, and it will be given to you: good measure, pressed down, shaken together, and running over will be put into your bosom. For with the same measure that you use, it will be measured back to you*" (Luke 6:38). God's emphasis is always on our receiving, not so much on our giving. Solomon's statement in Proverbs 3:10 about our barns being filled is an incredible statement. It all boils down to one question, "Who are we going to believe?"

We have the wisest advice ever given on stewardship by the wisest man who ever lived. He put it like this, "*Honor the Lord with your possessions, and with the firstfruits of all your increase; so your barns will be filled with plenty, and your vats will overflow with new wine*" (Prov. 3:9-10).

What is the purpose of our stewardship? Are we honoring God? What is the product of our stewardship? Are we simply trying to be a steward of our time and talent and not with our treasure? God said the product of our stewardship is "our possessions." What is the priority of our stewardship? Remember, the firstfruits belong to

Him. What is the promise of our stewardship? We can take Him at His Word. However, the real question is not if we ask ourselves these four questions, but if we will act upon them. If we have not been regular tithers, will we begin to do so now?

The greatest stewardship verse in all the Bible is found in John 3:16, "*For God so loved the world that He gave His only begotten Son, that whoever believes in Him should not perish but have everlasting life.*" The Lord Jesus was the product of the Father's stewardship to you. He was His only Son, the firstfruits of all those who would be born again after Him. We have a tremendous opportunity to honor God with our lives – the greatest of all our possessions. He said, "*Those who honor Me, I will honor*" (1 Sam. 2:30).

4

Love Isn't Afraid Of Giving Too Much

LUKE 21: 1–4 (NKJV™)
Nelson Price
President of 1987 Pastors' Conference

J esus Christ sat in the temple watching as time came for the offering. He observed who gave what. He saw the rich give. Some gave proportionately and with the proper attitude. However, there were those who gave demonstrably. Of them, He warned others, *"When you do a charitable deed, do not sound the trumpet as the hypocrites do in the temple"* (Matt. 6:2).

Christ had just concluded delivering a powerful message in the women's court of the Temple. In that message He denounced certain people for "devouring widow's houses." He then observes a poor widow come into the court. In the court there were thirteen trumpet shaped chests placed along the colonnades. Out from among the shadows of the colonnades emerged this poor widow. She had fought the dismal battle in the outback of poverty and won. She had come to offer the trophy of victory, her two mites.

To envision what He was speaking of, picture the RCA logo of the old record player with the trumpet shaped horn. The treasury box into which gifts were placed had a trumpet shaped opening. Some persons knew just how to throw a coin in to make it go around-and-around and make a ringing sound as it did. This was called "sounding the trumpet." It was a way some persons had of saying, "Look at me and see my big gift."

Jesus then turned His gaze on the widow who quietly put in two mites. Jesus said of her gift, "Truly I say to you that this poor widow has put in more than all: for all these out of their abundance have put in offerings for God, but she out of her poverty has put in all the livelihood that she had."

Several things are impressive about that story. One is Jesus had the audacity to observe what people were giving. He still does. Jesus even called the disciples over to focus their attention on her gift. Paul spoke of the gifts given by the church in Philippi as being credited to their "account" (Phil. 4:17). God keeps an "account" of our giving.

Another impressive fact is the size of the gift wasn't important. Her two mites were the equivalent of about one-quarter cent today. It is not equal gifts that count but rather equal sacrifice. Her sacrifice far exceeded that of any other person.

Come now to a more contemporary setting. Russian refugees are being asked to give to a fund to purchase Bibles to be sent back to their homeland where they are scarce. A quiet little lady who had been widowed by the marksmanship of a Russian border guard listened attentively. As the offering was received she responded joyously. "Here, take all my savings. It's everything I've got!" "No, no, that's too much," was the reply. "Take it anyway," she insisted, "Love isn't afraid of giving too much."

Love Isn't Afraid Of Giving Too Much!

That generosity indicts many of us. Candidly after hearing this, all of us would like to be known for such generosity. However, because of poor money management growing out of a lack of understanding of personal finance, many have boxed themselves in to the point they are so over committed they feel they can't give even though they would like to.

Christian pulpits are in part responsible for the plight of such people because money management hasn't been taught. The advertising agencies and lending institutions have done a better job of enticing people to spend than the church has in disciplining its members in money management. To put it another way, people need help in the matter of self-control.

Secular society has almost convinced us there is a clause in the Constitution guaranteeing us the right to "life, liberty, and the pursuit of excessive credit." As a result many persons have overused credit to purchase items that end up in carport sales.

Many people have become discouraged and given up on the idea of tithing. That can be overcome with a little resolve and a few lifestyle changes. It takes God aided discipline. That great philosopher Yogi Berra said, "a nickel ain't worth a dime anymore."

We have failed to develop the Biblical attitude of the young man who opened a bank account in Barwick, Georgia in the name of John W. Yates & Company. The teller asked, "Who owns the company?" Without hesitation the young man replied, "God! He gives me everything I have. I am just managing this money for Him." That is what stewardship is. It is managing for God whatever He has put under our supervision.

Fights over money are the number one cause of marital discord. It even ranks ahead of fights over what TV program to watch; more than a root canal. In our sex oriented society, fifty-six percent of us say there comes a point in every marriage when money becomes more important than sex.

Dr. Allan Scholom, a clinical psychologist in Chicago said, "There's absolutely no relationship between the amount of money one had and the amount one worries about it." In short, it's not how much you make but what you make of it.

Among eight touchy subjects brought up in a major nationwide survey, money was the one most Americans felt less comfortable discussing. It ranked ahead of those formerly considered taboo:

religion and politics.

Money equals image. More Americans said they had rather be rich than thinner, smarter, taller, more patient, or better looking.

Jesus knew we needed help in this regard. He used 38 parables to teach great truths. Twelve of them were on the subject of money.

Giving Is an Act of Obedience

When He spoke of the meticulous details given by the Pharisees about tithing, He said we "ought" to tithe. On another subject, I recently recounted for a friend what the Bible said on the subject we were discussing. She replied, "It doesn't say that but once." It doesn't say John 3:16 but once but the message is clear. Jesus' statement regarding the fact we "ought" to tithe is recorded twice in Matthew 23:23 and Luke 11:42. Jesus said, "*Why do you call Me 'Lord, Lord,' and do not do the things which I say?*" (Luke 6:46).

Why call an individual "boss" and not do what you are told to do? Why call a person "coach" and not run the plays prescribed? Why call a person "commander" and not obey the orders given? Why call Christ, Savior, Master and Lord and not do what He says do?

In ALL things we should predetermine what God defines as His course of action and follow it.

We can do anything Christ has instructed us to do. "*I can do all things through Christ who strengthens me*" (Phil. 4:13). A modern translation renders this: "*I can do everything God asks me to do…*" Everything? Everything!

He never asks us to do anything He won't enable us to do. If you say, "You don't understand, we just can't afford to tithe," you are revealing you have your priorities wrong. God has given you the resources to tithe. You need to reallocate them.

Our spirit in giving is defined for us this way: *"So let each one give as he purposes in his heart, not grudgingly or of necessity; for God loves a cheerful giver"* (2 Cor. 9:7).

In Austin, Texas a wealthy Texan who gives more than $5,000,000 a year to the cause of Christ was asked if he thought certain new tax laws would hurt charitable giving. He replied, "No! If a person has it in his heart to give, no law will keep him from giving and if he doesn't have it in his heart to give, no law will motivate him to give." He was saying, we give as we "purpose" in our heart.

Giving Is A Testimony

Nearly 2,000 years have passed since that widow gave her two mites and her testimony still inspires us. The unselfish act by this poor widow was a meaningful and refreshing testimony to Christ. It came during the last week of His life, the dismal Passion Week. This tender scene came amid priestly frowns, studied cruelty, injustice, and treachery. She came like a refreshing breeze out of the desert of poverty, gave her gift and like a thin mist vanished. Her testimony was complete. She in her act of giving all of her living had cheered the heart of the one on His way to give all His living. The sound of those two small mites entering the trumpet will follow Him all through Pilate's judgment hall, the mocking crowd, and to the hill. Her testimony would encourage Him through His travail.

In the "Vision of Sir Launfal" a character named Lowell says:
>"Not what we give, but what we share,
>For the gift without the giver is bare;
>Who gives himself with his alms feeds three,
>Himself, his hungering neighbor, and Me."

In our giving, as with the widow's gift, we provide for three: ourselves, the needy, and the Lord. We earn money. We exchange our time and efforts for it. Thus, it becomes a symbol of ourselves. When we give it, we are giving testimony that we have given ourselves. We can each say, "Money is a symbol of me. In giving the prescribed amount, I am bearing testimony I have given myself."

When God blessed Abraham with conquest of the Promised Land, the first thing Abraham did was tithe. At that time there was no law requiring the tithe. Tithing predates the law. In doing so, Abraham gave testimony that he had given himself to the Lord and acknowledged God's ownership.

That was the purpose in instituting the tithe. It gives opportunity to obey the Lord and thereby acknowledge Him as owner of everything.

Giving Meets One Of Our Basic Needs

The temple was the setting when Christ observed the widow giving her two mites. The temple was plated with gold and had furnishings of fine brass. Obviously her little coins were not needed, BUT she needed to give. It was her nature.

A sacrificial spirit is part of the new nature of a Christian. It is a characteristic of our Heavenly Father. Jesus said when you give, people acknowledge you are "children" of the Father. If this trait of the Father is unfulfilled, a person feels guilty.

We should not limit our giving to simply tithing. There are other admirable causes needing financial support. Some persons excuse themselves for not giving the basic tithe to the church by saying they give to support a relative, or another good cause, or to a building program. Those are admirable things to do.

In the Old Testament where we have many examples of giving, they gave the tithes as required. They being an agricultural society also provided for the poor and needy additionally. They left grain in the corners of the fields and along the edges for the poor to come and harvest. They left fruit on the trees for them to harvest. This was all in addition to their tithes. Our giving should consist of tithing plus.

Psychologists say a part of a person's therapy is paying. It meets an innate need to give. It relieves guilt. Psychologists are merely confirming what Christ taught when He said, "*It is more blessed to give than to receive*" (Acts 20: 35).

Love Isn't Afraid Of Giving Too Much!

Our model of priorities in giving was defined by the impoverished Macedonian church of which it was said, "*They first gave themselves*" (2 Cor. 8:5).

Walt Whitman, considered by many as America's all-time official poet laureate, often wrote of the wonder of America. He once said, "When I give, I do not give lectures or a little charity. When I give, I give myself."

Only when we truly give ourselves to Christ can our other giving be proper. When we do really give ourselves to Him, our giving is proper and is a testimony of our giving of self to Him.

Love Isn't Afraid Of Giving Too Much!

In giving her two mites, the widow taught a simple but significant lesson regarding total commitment. She did not give because her purse was full but because her heart was full of love.

When you give yourself to Christ, you still haven't given too much. Love prompts us to give ourself to Him. What that widow did that encouraged Christ was give a gift of love. The two coins just represented the love.

5

What's In It For Me?
Six Myths About Tithing
Malachi 3:7-10 (NKJV™)
Stan Coffey
President of 1988 Pastors' Conference

Everything we do in this life has an impact on eternity, how you will spend eternity, how you will enjoy eternity. Whether it is giving a cup of cold water in Jesus' name or if it is going to the mission field, whether it is something big or something small, every act of kindness that we do in the name of the Lord in His glory out of love for Him, will be remembered by Him and will be rewarded by Him.

"What's in it for me" is a question the disciples raised when they left everything they had and answered the call to follow Jesus. The fishermen left their nets; Matthew left his tax collector's desk; others left their occupations and they left it all and they just followed Jesus. One day Peter said, *"Lord we have left all and followed Thee, what shall we have therefore?"* And Jesus said, *"No man has left houses or land, or husbands or wives, or brothers or sisters and followed Me who will not have a hundred fold in this life and the life to come."*

So what's in it for me? One thing, eternal life is in it for you if you follow Jesus. That ought to be enough but not only does He give eternal life, but He gives a reward to us. And that is a fascinating thing that Jesus is going to give to us on top of eternal life, a reward in heaven. If I become a faithful, biblical giver, what will be in it for me? How does it benefit me if I tithe? It looks like I am just 10% less better off if I tithe. I am just 10% poorer if I give a tithe on Sunday morning. So what is in it for me? How in the world can it benefit me if I tithe?

One of the reasons people don't understand the tithe is because there are a lot of myths about the tithe, a lot of misconceptions about the tithe. I want to put some of those misconceptions to rest and I want to motivate you if I can by telling you what is in it for you by showing you those misconceptions and exposing some of the lies that the devil has put out there about the tithe.

Malachi 3:7-10 *"Yet from the days of your fathers You have gone away from My ordinances and have not kept them. Return to Me, and I will return to you," Says the LORD of hosts. "But you said, 'In what way shall we return?' "Will a man rob God? Yet you have robbed Me! But you say, 'In what way have we robbed You?' In tithes and offerings. You are cursed with a curse, For you have robbed Me, even this whole nation. Bring all the tithes into the storehouse, that there may be food in My house, and try Me now in this..."*

Giving begins with a tenth. The word tithe literally means a tenth part. It means one tenth. God makes it very plain that the beginning point of giving begins with the tenth part. In the Old Testament if they had ten cows, they gave one cow to God. If they had ten pounds of grain, they gave one pound to God. If they had ten measures of flour, they gave one measure to God. This was the tradition and the command of God from the very beginning.

There is something that is happening in Christianity today. The percentage of giving in Christianity is becoming less and less. In fact, there has been a 27-year decline in giving in churches as a whole. 1.5% to 3.5% is the average that God's people give to Christian work across the board. 17% of Christians say that they give a tithe, but in reality about 3% of Christians tithe to their church. You can understand why we have great needs on the mission field. We have missionaries who are willing to go but we don't have the money to send the missionaries.

Only 3% of God's people actually tithe. 30% to 50% of church attendees have blank giving records. 30% to 50% give nothing whatsoever. And 70% of Christians leave nothing to their church or to God's work when they die, because many of them do not have a will in place. Others do not think to leave anything in their estate to the work of God.

I know many people don't tithe because they don't have a biblical concept of giving or they have listened to some of the misconceptions about giving that are out there. Tithing is not popular or even politically correct. You always run the risk of offending visitors if you talk about giving on Sunday mornings. Yet this is a part of God's Word and it is an integral part of what the Christian life is all about.

It is all about giving. The giving of self, the giving of talents, and the giving of resources. Jesus was all about giving. That is why He came to this world, to give Himself a ransom for many. You cannot be a Christian without having a giving heart. That is what being a believer is all about. What are some of these myths about giving?

Myth One: Tithing Is An Option

The first myth is that tithing is an option for a believer. Now you are not saved by works, but God gives certain commands that are expected after you are saved. For instance, baptism is not an option. You are commanded to be baptized. Baptism doesn't save you but it is commanded of you after you believe to be baptized. That is a command of God. Tithing is just as much a command as is baptism. You are commanded to be a tither. God commands that in His Word. In Malachi 3 He says, *"Bring ye all the tithes into the storehouse."*

That is in the imperative. He doesn't say, "Bring it if you would like to or bring it if it feels good, or bring it if you would agree with Me." God says, "Bring it." It is a command of God. Now many believers seem to think this is an option. I can check this box if I want to or I can ignore it. It doesn't mean that you will go to hell if you don't tithe but it just means you cannot be an obedient believer. You cannot enjoy certain blessings and you cannot get in on certain benefits if you are not a tither.

You say, what is in it for me? You are going to see that there are many blessings that are in it for you but you simply cannot have those blessings unless you are obedient. Jesus said, *"If you love Me, keep My commandments."* God says, "Listen I own everything. I own 100%. I own you. I own everything about you. I own all the money. I own 100% of it. And I require that as a beginning point you give back to Me 10% to show that you understand that it all comes from Me."

In Deuteronomy, we read that Moses told the people that the purpose of tithing was to show that you put God first in your life. That is the purpose of the whole thing. So tithing is not an option. To think tithing is optional is just a myth.

Now you remember the story of David. He had it in his heart to build the temple. He wanted to do that so badly for God because he was a man after God's own heart and yet David had been a man of war. God told David that he could not build this temple because he had blood on his hands, but that his son Solomon would build the temple. He is going to be a man of peace, but you will raise the money to build the temple before you die. And that is exactly what David did. David gave a substantial amount of money to build the temple and here is what he said in 1 Chronicles 29:14 *"But who am I, and who are my people, that we should be able to offer so willingly as this? For all things come from you, and of your own we have given you."* He is saying, "God, what we give to You is already Yours." It's like, we take it from the hand of God and we place it into the hand of God. It all began with God. It all belongs to God and when we give, we are simply giving back to God who gave it to us. That is another purpose of tithing; to show God that we recognize where it comes from.

You may have developed industriousness in your life. You may have a great work ethic. You may have developed your talents. That is commendable. God will reward you for that. But God gave you the ability to get wealth. The Scripture says it is God who gives you the ability to get wealth. So it all came from Him. Tithing is not an option.

Myth Two: Tithing Was Under The Law, But Under Grace It Does Not Apply To Us

There is a myth that says tithing was under the law but under grace we don't need to tithe. It doesn't apply to us. Let me show you something about tithing. Tithing commenced before the law.

In Genesis 14 before the law was given, we meet a man named Melchizedek who was a priest of God. Now many believe that Melchizedek was a pre-incarnate appearance of Jesus. I believe the Bible teaches this and confirms it in the book of Hebrews. Abraham had fought a battle and he had many spoils from the battle. This mysterious priest of the Lord met Abram as he was returning from battle and Abram paid a tithe of all the spoils from the battle to Melchizedek. Genesis 14:18-20, "*Then Melchizedek, king of Salem, brought out bread and wine; he was the priest of God Most High. And he blessed him and said: 'Blessed be Abram of God Most High. Possessor of heaven and earth; and blessed be God Most High, who has delivered your enemies into your hand.' And he gave him a tithe of all.*" Now you only give your tithe to God. The book of Hebrews, the New Testament reference, indicates that it was as though Abram was giving a tithe to Jesus Christ Himself who was a priest after the order of Melchizedek. The point is that the law had not been given but Abram practiced tithing.

The tithe continued during the law. In Leviticus, we read that the tithe is holy unto the Lord. Holy means set apart. Holy means you don't put your hands on it. Holy means it belongs to God. If something is holy, it is set apart. It is sanctified to God.

Then the tithe was commended after the law. In Matthew 23:23, the only thing that Jesus ever commended the Pharisees for was tithing. He criticized them for a lot of things but He didn't criticize them for tithing, He commended them for tithing. Matthew 23:23 says, "*Woe to you, scribes and Pharisees, hypocrites! For you pay tithe of mint and anise and cumin, and have neglected the weightier matters of the law: Justice and mercy and faith. These you ought to have done without leaving the others undone.*" He says you pay tithe of the mint and the anise and the cumin. You pay the tithe of even these little herbs. You are so careful to tithe on the smallest thing but you neglect the weightier matters. He said you should have paid the tithe. Jesus commended the Pharisees for tithing after the law was given and during the time Jesus was on earth. So you cannot get out of tithing by saying, "Well, tithing was during the Old Testament but it doesn't apply to us." Tithing under grace ought to be the beginning point not the ending point.

Myth Three: I Can't Afford To Tithe

I will grant you, sometimes you think you can't afford to tithe. Both spouses are working, trying to meet the bills and needs of their children, maybe two or three are in college. Then there are credit cards and high interest rates. I know it is hard to tithe. I know the devil makes you think, "Man, I just can't afford to tithe. Maybe when I can afford it." Let me tell you, that is a myth that the devil tries to sell you to keep you from getting God's blessing.

The truth is you can't afford NOT to tithe. Now I know it seems hard. The hardest time in our lives to tithe was when we made $60 a week. In my first church I made $50 a week as pastor and $10 a week as janitor. And I was a better janitor than I was a preacher. It was difficult to tithe then. Glenda made a little more than that but not much more working as a teller at the bank. But that was all the income we had and I was in college, on top of that. I didn't have a momma and daddy who paid my tuition. I was paying college tuition. I was pastoring a church and I was driving 85 miles one way, three times a week and living on the church field. But we were committed to tithe.

I made it through school with hardly any debt whatsoever and God supplied our needs. We had the blessing of being able to go through school and to give honor and credit and glory to God for His provision. The truth is you can't afford not to tithe. The reason is you give God His tithe and you become partners with God. When you become partners with God, your bills become God's problem. When you become partners with God, He begins to help you solve your problems. He begins to help guide and direct your decisions. He begins to help guide your financial decisions.

I promise you, you will not do more with 100% of your money without God than you will with God at 90%. It makes more sense to have God on your side and 90% of your money than you doing it without God and 100% of your money.

Now that is why in verse 10 He said, "*I will open the windows of heaven and pour out such blessing there will not be room enough to receive it.*" So don't go out of here saying, "The preacher just asked for money. I knew that is what he would do. It was my first time to come and he asks for money." Listen to this so you won't say that. What will God do for you? He will restore your prayer life because you are being obedient to Him and that barrier is out of the way. He will release His power. He said, "*I will open the windows of heaven.*" That means He will restore your prayer life. "*He will pour out blessings upon you*" means He will release His power and He will pour the Holy Spirit in your life. He will open the windows of heaven and pour out His spirit upon you.

Furthermore, He will rebuke the devourer that is Satan. The devourer wants to cause marriage problems. The devourer wants to cause family problems. The devourer wants to cause financial problems. The devourer wants to wreck and ruin your life any way he can. He is your enemy. He is your adversary. But God says, "Be faithful to Me, prove Me, test Me." He said, "Bring the tithe into the storehouse and see if I will not rebuke the devourer for your sake. I will rebuke Satan."

That is why you can't afford not to tithe. It is not because you will get a check in the mail next week. It is because He will rebuke the devourer away from you. I don't know about you, but I want God on my side and I want Satan rebuked away from my family and away from my children and away from my life. That is what God says He will do for you.

Myth Four: The Tithe Is All God Expects

Is tithing all God expects? God says, "You have robbed Me in tithes and offerings." In Old Testament times, they not only had the tithe but they had the meal offering and the grain offering. They had all kinds of offerings.

Today in our churches, we have offerings over and above the tithe. Our church has two offerings. In the past, we had three offerings. We have an offering in the middle of the service and an offering at the end of the service.

As you begin to tithe and as you begin to grow in giving, many times, God will impress you to give beyond the tithe. He said, "You robbed Me of tithes and offerings." The tithe is the minimum not the maximum. The tithe is the beginning of giving not the end. The tithe is not the ceiling. It is the floor. The tithe is not the stopping place. It is the starting place.

As you grow in your giving, you will see that God will enable you and bless you so that you can give over and above the tithe. You can give offerings above the tithe.

J.L. Kraft, the founder of Kraft Foods, was a tremendous giver who gave way beyond the tithe, he was asked, "Do you believe in tithing?" He said, "No, I don't believe in tithing though it is a good beginning place."

Myth Five: I May Give My Tithe Anywhere I Choose

The fifth myth is I may give my tithe wherever I want. Well, this verse says, "*Bring your whole tithe into the storehouse.*" The temple of that day had a storehouse because they tithed agricultural products. They tithed sheep, cows, bulls, pigeons, grain, wheat, and corn. At the temple, they had all these graineries. They had all these pens to hold all the things that people brought in tithe. So they brought their tithe to the storehouse.

We have a bank account. The storehouse today is the local New Testament church. The local New Testament church is how God gets the work done. Every para-church ministry owes its life to the local New Testament church. It is the local New Testament church that teaches people, wins people, trains people to give, trains people in discipleship, and that makes it possible for other ministries to exist.

It is fine and good to give offerings beyond the tithe to all those other ministries, but the tithe belongs in your church. D. James Kennedy or any other television preacher is not going to come when you need somebody to bury your loved one. John Hagee is not going to come when you are sick or in the hospital. It is your local New Testament church that is going to give counsel. James Robinson is not going to come.

Your tithe belongs to your church. Who won you to Christ? Who baptized you? Who was there when you had a need? If you want to give over and above to those ministries as God leads you, fine. But your tithe belongs to your church.

Paul made a play on this word when he wrote in 1 Corinthians 16:2, "*On the first day of the week let everyone of you lay by in* store, *as God hath prospered him.*" He made a play on words when he said lay by in store. It is almost the same word as the storehouse in the Old Testament. He was using that as a figure of speech to remind them of what they did in the Old Testament. On the first day of the week, let everyone of you '*lay by in store*'.

Myth Six: We Should Not Expect A Reward When We Give

Here is another myth. That we should not expect a reward when we give. Now that is what you have been told all your life but that is not right. You should *expect* a reward when you give.

What's in it for me? There is a lot in it for you. I have already mentioned that God will open the windows of heaven, but He says here, "*Try Me here in this.*" This is the only promise in the Bible that tells you to prove the existence of God. God said prove Me or try Me. "*If I will not open the windows of heaven and pour you out a blessing that there will not be room enough to receive it and I will rebuke the devourer for your sake.*" God says, "I will reward you for this."

There are many other verses. In Luke 6:38, Jesus says, "*Give and it shall be given unto you; good measure shaken down, running over, shall men give unto your bosom.*" There is a principle in the Bible: to receive you have to give, to gain you have to lose. Jesus said, "*Unless a corn of wheat die, it abides alone; but if it dies it will bring forth much fruit.*" This is a principle in Scripture. In order for your gift to grow, it has to be given away.

There is much to gain by giving. There is nothing to gain by hoarding. There is nothing to gain by keeping but there is much to gain by giving. You ought to give, expecting God to do what He says He will do.

In Philippians 4:19, Paul is writing to the Philippians and he is saying, "Thank you for writing to me, thank you for sending me a gift while I was in prison." He said, "You are the only church that remembered that I was in a deep dark hole. Out of all the churches I served, out of all the people I won to Christ, out all the people I preached to, everyone else forgot me. I was down in this deep dark hole in Rome and you remembered me and you sent me a gift." And he said, "I will tell you what is going to happen to you, '*My God shall supply all your need according to His riches in glory by Christ Jesus.*'"

This promise wasn't given in abstract. That promise wasn't given in a vacuum. Read the context. It was given to a church that was faithful to remember the apostle Paul and to give to him. To that church he said, "*My God shall supply all your need.*" This promise is made to people who gave and who were faithful to think of someone else. They were unselfish. They were caring and they gave. Paul said, "Because you have supplied my need, God will supply your need."

I never worry about the money I give away. When I feel impressed of God to give to some person that I don't even know but they have a need, I give money to them. I never worry about that because I know God is going to meet my need. When I have an opportunity to give to help somebody, I never worry about it if God impresses me to give because I know God is going to meet my need. That is what He said He would do.

So all through the Scripture, the Bible says, "God will supply back to you." And not just financial rewards. God will give you many other kinds of rewards. The money you put in this church has brought thousands to Christ. I want to tell you, one day when you stand before Jesus, you will be so glad that God used you. God doesn't look at the amount you give, God looks at the amount you have left. God doesn't look at a person and say, "This was a huge gift."

You remember the widow who gave all she had. Jesus was watching people as they gave and the widow came and all she had was less than a penny and she gave it. It was all she had to live on. Jesus had watched all the wealthy give and they gave their great amounts and then this widow came and gave her mite. Jesus said, "*I want to tell you, this woman has given more than they all.*" Don't think that your gift is ever insignificant. God will reward you for what you give and God will bless you in this life and in the life to come.

The greatest gift of all was the gift of Jesus. He came down from glory. He lived the perfect life. They lied about Him, they spit upon Him, they abused Him, they beat Him upon the face, they crowned Him with a crown of thorns and they beat His back with a cat-of-nine-tails. You could hardly recognize His face. They nailed Him to the cross and He hung on that cross for six hours. The world grew dark, the thunder rolled, there was a great earthquake and the temple veil was torn from top to bottom. He cried out on the cross, "*My God, My God, why hast thou forsaken Me?*"

My sin and your sin was placed upon Him. He was separated from the Father as He shed His blood as a payment for our sin. "*God so loved the world that He gave His only begotten Son that if we would believe in Him we would not perish but have everlasting life.*"

This is the greatest gift that we could ever receive. The Bible says that if you will believe on Him and are willing to confess Him as your Lord and Savior, you will not die but have everlasting life. I pray that you will open your heart and accept Him and receive Him as the greatest gift of all. God wants your life. God wants your heart. God wants you to accept Jesus into your life. That is why Jesus came and gave His life for you.

6

Why Every Christian Should Practice Tithing...at Least

MALACHI 3: 7-12 NASB

Thomas D. Elliff

President of 1990 Pastors' Conference

When a pastor stands before his congregation to proclaim the Word of God, he is often required to perform a role quite similar to that of an attorney arguing his case before a jury. Using all the evidence at his disposal, he urges his congregational "jury" to make the proper verdict. So today I want you to think of me in that sense. I want to make the case that every Christian should practice tithing, at the very least, and I want to urge you to make what, for some, will be a life-changing verdict.

Today, I am praying that, by God's grace, every true believer here will move up in your understanding of the tithe, then choose to move forward in faith as you embrace a truly biblical concept of stewardship.

Now it is important for me to define those whom I consider to be in the jury box today. Let's see if you qualify!

I want to argue my case, first and foremost, before those of you who are genuinely children of God. Having repented of sin and believed in Christ, you have been born again unto eternal life. Because the Holy Spirit lives within you, you have the capacity to perceive what God is saying through His Word. Are you absolutely certain that you are saved?

But this jury must be even more strictly defined. It must be a jury comprised of genuine Christians who are absolutely convinced that the Word of God is infallible, without error, and totally inspired of God. Can you sit on such a jury? Are you willing to accept the teachings in this book as true? What's more, are you willing to embrace the teachings of God's Word as your own standard for living?

I cannot argue this case effectively before a jury that regards the teachings of God's Word as interesting but not applicable to their own lives. You can only sit on this jury if you are willing to say, "Preacher, if I find without doubt that there is something God wants me to do, some way in which God desires an alteration in my behavior, then by God's grace, I will immediately embrace that truth and act upon it." Do you qualify to sit on this jury?

With our jury defined and selected, let me turn to the matter before us. **Does God's Word actually encourage God's children to practice tithing…at the very least?**

While we will examine Scriptures in both the Old and New Testaments, I'd like for you to first open your Bible to the Book of Malachi. Listen to the voice of the man who sounded the final prophetic word of the Old Testament. When his voice dies out, the Scriptures will go silent for four hundred years. The next voice we would hear would be that of John the Baptizer, announcing the arrival of the Messiah. Malachi, as his name suggests, is God's "messenger." We must listen carefully to what he says.

God Is The One Who Desires The Tithe

"*Bring the whole tithe into the storehouse*," writes Malachi, "*so that there may be food in My house…*" (3:10a). Here Malachi is writing on behalf of *The LORD of Hosts* (10b), maintaining his own humble position as God's "messenger boy." In these few words God addresses five basic issues of tithing. Consider:

1. The principle of tithing. In both the Old and New Testaments, the tithe is considered the first ten percent, set aside for the purposes of God. It never refers to substance that is "left over," but always indicates a deliberate choice, an act of faith in God's ability to supply all that we need. *"Honor the Lord from your wealth, and from the first of all your produce."* We read in Proverbs 3:9-10, *"So your barns will be filled with plenty and your vats will overflow with new wine."*

2. The place of tithing. Here we read that the tithe is to be brought to the storehouse. The tithe, in other words, was not considered a resource to be spread around at an individual's discretion, but a specific, set aside amount, brought to the house of God. We will see later why this is so important.

3. The punctuality of tithing. In the Old Testament, we read of specific times during the year when the tithe was to be brought to the Temple. Now, in this New Testament era, we are not without some instruction regarding our giving. The apostle Paul, for instance, when writing to the believers in Corinth about an offering for the poor (not to be confused with the tithe), gives us some insight (1 Cor. 16:2). *"Now concerning the collection for the saints, as I have directed the churches of Galatia, so do you also. On the first day of the week each one of you is to put aside and save, so that no collections be made when I come."* Paul's idea of stewardship was that it was to be a systematic, definite commitment. I have discovered that many who do not at least tithe in that fashion, do not actually end up tithing at all.

4. The purpose of tithing. Tithing provides an opportunity to express faith in the Lord by obedience to His commands. When someone says, "But I cannot afford to tithe," they are ignoring two facts: 1) *"Without faith it is impossible to please God"* (Heb. 11:6); and 2) This is why the tithe is a percentage, not an amount. But more was intended than the mere placing of material substance in the storehouse of God! It was through the bringing of the tithe that the people of God were brought under the Word of God on a systematic basis. When God's people brought the tithe, they were provided the opportunity to grow in the knowledge of the Lord, and worship Him.

5. *The practice of tithing.* Many object to the tithe because they consider it to be merely an Old Testament practice. While a believer under grace should always exceed in practice what the Law demanded, we must understand that the scope of tithing far exceeds the Law.

Tithing was practiced at least four hundred years before the giving of the Law. The vivid account in Genesis 14 of Abraham's rescue of Lot states that in the process of rescue, Abraham met with Melchizedek and paid tithes to him of all he had. The New Testament review of that event (Heb. 7) clearly states that Melchizedek was a type of Christ, and that Abraham's tithes bore remarkable significance for those who followed him. In Genesis 28:16-22, we find Jacob, arising from his dream at Bethel, erecting a memorial and saying *"This stone, which I have set up as a pillar, will be God's house, and of all that You give me I will surely give a tenth to You."*

Tithing was commanded in the Law. Most of us are aware of this fact, but listen to God's words in Leviticus 27:30: *"And all the tithe of the land, whether of the seed or the land, or the fruit of the tree IS THE LORD'S. IT IS HOLY UNTO THE LORD."* When Nehemiah discovered that the people of God had been dilatory in bringing their tithes, he immediately reprimanded the leaders and called for a restoration of tithing (Neh.13:10-14).

Tithing was reinforced by Christ, as recorded in the New Testament (Matt. 23:23). After noting that the Scribes and Pharisees practiced tithing to the ultimate degree, Christ said, *"This you ought to have done, and not neglected the weightier provisions of the law."* Christ, in other words, expected more from them than merely tithing. If you will carefully read Christ's Sermon on the Mount (Matt. 5-7), you will discover that Christ expects *more* of His followers than was ever demanded by the law. Christ even notes that there is great danger for anyone who teaches others to break the Law (5:16-19).

One third of Christ's parables refer to the stewardship of our resources. One verse out of every six verses in the Gospels refers to our stewardship of resources. Approximately twenty percent of the entire Bible is in some way related to stewardship issues. Since the Lord obviously cares how we steward our resources, surely those of us who are Christ-followers would want to practice tithing… **at least.**

God Describes The Non-Tither

Tithing is such an important issue to God that He goes to great pains to describe those who did not follow this practice under the Law. His description should give pause to anyone who, under grace, does not practice tithing as a minimum expression of faith.

1. The non-tither is a rebel (v.7). When rebellious children are confronted with the consequences of their behavior, you will often hear them respond with questions. "What?" they will remonstrate. "What did I do?" Listen to the words of the prophet: *"From the days of your fathers you have turned aside from My statutes and have not kept them. Return to Me and I will return to you," says the LORD of Host. "But you say, 'How shall we return?' "Will a man rob God? Yet you are robbing Me! But you say, 'How have we robbed You?' In tithes and offerings."* Can you not hear the rebellion in their voices?

2. The non-tither is a robber (v.8). Malachi, God's messenger, is unrelenting in his charges as he delivers God's message. *"You are cursed with a curse, for you are robbing Me, the whole nation of you!"* It is just as much a theft *not* to put into the offering plate what belongs to God, as it is to *take* from the offering plate what does not belong to you. Non-tithers are not merely careless or down on their luck. They are robbers!

3. The non-tither will reap the results of his disobedience (9). Think what it meant to be "*cursed with a curse.*" It meant to live without God's blessing on your life. In the verses that follow we are given to understand that the disobedient children of God were experiencing a life that could only be described as hard, without God's provision or protection. Ironically, some will use the very lean-ness of their circumstances to justify further lack of faith and disobedience. Life becomes a vicious cycle that can only be broken by confession, repentance and faithful obedience.

God Is The One Who Delights In Those Who Tithe…At Least

"*Bring the whole tithe into the storehouse, so that there may be food in My house, and test Me now in this,*" *says the LORD of hosts, 'if I will not open for you the windows of heaven and pour out for you a blessing until it overflows. Then will I rebuke the devourer for you, so that it will not destroy the fruits of the ground; nor will your vine in the field cast its grapes,' says the LORD of hosts. 'All the nations will call you blessed, for you shall be a delightful land,' says the LORD of hosts*" (vss. 10-12).

You would not call your house payment a "gift" to the bank. And neither would the bank! You are only providing what belongs to them. You owe it! Similarly, the tithe is the Lord's. Neither the tithe, nor anything short of a tithe should be called a gift. You cannot *give* until you have first rendered up what is *owed*. God wants His children to enter into the utter joys of giving. But first you must tithe. Here God is inviting you to put Him to the test by tithing…**at least.**

Notice what God promises to those who tithe…**at least.**

1. Plenty (v.10). The very fact that so many who *profess* to be Christians also *confess* to be "scarcely making it," is a revelation of our true state of disobedience. While tithing is not the *only* principle involved in good stewardship, it *is* the foremost principle. Apart from that, an individual has turned away from the life of faith, a faith without which one cannot please God.

To the tither, God says, "*I will open up the windows of heaven and pour out a blessing.*" This blessing is not the accumulation of mere "stuff." Scripture reminds us that the "*Blessing of the Lord, it makes rich, and He adds no sorrow with it*" (Prov. 10:22). Now that is blessing indeed!

2. Protection (v.11). A careful reading of verse 11 indicates that God will not only protect our *actual* resources, but our *anticipated* resources as well. That is an insurance policy worth more than money can buy! From his position of faith in God, the tither can expect the Lord's providence to be in force, and live free of worry. After all, by his faithful practice of the tithe he has indicated that all he has is in God's hands.

3. Praise (v.12). "*All the nations will call you blessed, for you shall be a delightful land…*" Not only will believers and unbelievers alike see the blessing of God on your life, they will say you are blessed! Your life will become a testimony to God's mighty providence!

Time For The Verdict!

Having the blessing of being reared in a Christian home, I can honestly say I cannot recall a time when I did not tithe…**at least**. But as an eighteen-year-old student pastor, one memorable experience moved tithing from a mere "cerebral" acknowledgement to a lifetime of "heartfelt" practice.

Our church was in a stewardship campaign that involved a "pastoral visit" to the home of each church member. My wise pastor invited me along to the home of a delightfully engaging elderly gentleman, Bro. Ray Owens, a deacon in our church. "Bro

Ray," said the pastor dutifully, "You know we are in a stewardship campaign, and we are visiting all our members to encourage them to tithe. So that's why we are here."

"Now pastor," replied Bro. Ray with a twinkle in his eye, "You know I've always believed in *giving*. So when this campaign came along I decided to figure just how much I've been giving. I'm happy to report that my giving is about twice what my tithing would be. But I decided I'd do just what my pastor asked. So do you want me to tithe….or give?"

With that last statement, Bro. Ray's mouth turned up into a mischievous grin. "Come on, pastor! What'll it be?"

After several seconds of silence, the pastor looked up at his trusted friend and said, "Just give Bro. Ray, give!"

Bro. Ray had discovered a great secret of the Christian life. There's nothing quite so exciting as entering into the arena of giving. But that exciting arena is reserved for those who first tithe…**at least**.

So now I urge you, the jury, to make your verdict. And I feel safe in doing so! After all, you are genuinely born again. You believe the Bible is the inerrant Word of God. You have committed to immediately altering your life to conform to whatever God shows you to be His desire.

Now, will you decide to tithe…**at least**? I think you will.

7

The Power Of Ten

MALACHI 3:8-10
James Merritt
President of 1995 Pastors' Conference

For the last four weeks I have done something that I have never done before in my ministry and quite frankly, I am ashamed of it. For the first time in my ministry, I have actually preached an entire series of messages on the topic of money – stuff – wealth – possessions or the modern day term "bling." I am sure that there are those who skipped out on some of these messages when they found out what it was about. I wouldn't be surprised if there have not been others who have walked in and left saying things such as, "I knew it. All he wants is my money." or "All this church talks about is money."

I would just like to say a couple of things in response to that kind of thinking. If I were to preach a series of messages on how to have a strong marriage, would you expect me to apologize for it? If I were to preach a series of messages on how to be a good parent and raise responsible children, would you expect me to apologize for it? If I were to preach a series of messages on prayer and how to connect with God, on the Bible and how to understand scripture, on faith and how to trust God and receive the blessings of God, would you expect me to apologize? Of course the answer to that would be "no." Why is it that people expect a pastor to be almost apologetic when it comes to the matter of managing money God's way and giving so you can get in on God's blessing for your life? It doesn't matter whether I am preaching on marriage, raising children, handling your emotions or managing your money. The reason we preach these things is because we are trying to help you live a more joyful, fulfilled, blessed and abundant life.

As far as talking about money, I realize there are people who believe that money should never be mentioned in the church and that the church talks too much about it. Can I be very frank and honest? I want to apologize to you, because I haven't talked to you enough about it. Did you know that the Bible has about 500 verses on prayer, but over 2,350 verses on how to handle your money? Did you know there are 126 different biblical principles on finances and managing money in the New Testament alone? Did you know that Jesus talked more about money that He did about heaven and hell?

The Bible has much to say about money matters, because money matters. Money matters to you, because you need it. Money matters to God because He owns it. Money matters to Satan, because he wants it and that is why God has a plan for you and money. He has a plan on how you are to accumulate money, how you should assimilate money and how you should allocate money.

I am going to share with you today the single most powerful financial principle that I have ever found in the Bible. It is directly from the mind and the heart of God Himself. I don't make a lot of money-back guarantees, but I am going to make one to you today. If you will follow this one biblical principle, you will not only become an instant better manager of your money than you are right now, but God will instantly become a partner with you in your financial future and you can get an eternal rate of return on your money that you can't find on Wall Street or anywhere else. I call it "**The power of ten**." The power often is found in one simple word – "tithe." The word tithe simply means "tenth."

You are going to see, in a passage of scripture today, where God doesn't mince words, stammer or stutter, equivocate or hesitate that if you will commit to giving God the first ten percent of everything you earn, and everything that He gives you, He will unleash the power of ten in your life that will enable you to do more with your money than you ever dreamed possible. What is the power of ten?

It Is The Power To Be In God's Will

The passage that we are about to read in the last book of the Old Testament was written by, probably, the most unpopular preacher in the history of Israel. The book of Malachi is unusual in that the prophet Malachi uses the Socratic method of making his point.

If you remember, Socrates used to teach by asking questions. Every time he asked a question of the nation of Israel, it was always one that called for them to condemn themselves. Of all the questions he asked, this is perhaps the most amazing question ever asked in the Bible. "*Will a man rob God? Yet you are robbing Me! But you say, 'How have we robbed You?' In tithes and offerings*" (Mal. 3:8, NASB).

We all know it is one thing to charge someone with a crime, but it is another thing to prove it. Like most people accused of a crime, the initial response was to plead innocent. They said, "*In what way have we robbed God?*" In effect, they were saying, "Do you have any witnesses? Is there a smoking gun? What is your evidence?" The reply sent the entire nation into a stunned silence when God gives out His one piece of evidence – "in tithes and offerings."

Let me tell you why this had happened. They had forgotten two things. They had forgotten something about God and they had forgotten something about money. What they had forgotten about God was that God was keeping the books. God was checking the ledger. God was watching every time they wrote out a check or they transferred funds. God was watching everyone to see who was giving to His work and who wasn't. The ushers didn't see it. The pastor didn't know it. The finance ministry team couldn't prove it, but every time the people came together to worship, people were robbing God.

They weren't doing it with a gun. They weren't taking something when nobody was looking because you can steal in one of two ways. You can steal by taking something that does not belong to you or you can steal by keeping something that belongs to somebody else. I don't know who you are and I don't know where you sit, but if the Scripture is true, then every week in our church, when the basket is passed, there are people who rob God. It is not because they take something out of the basket, but because they don't put anything in the basket and God sees that and God notes that and God realizes that.

They had also forgotten something about money. They had forgotten that their money was not their money; it belonged to God. The tithe was meant to be a reminder to the people who gave it that God owns it all. He owns the fields. He owns the crops. He owns the livestock. He owns the silver. He owns the gold. He owns the real estate. He owns the checking account and God's tithe and what it represents is so important that when you don't give it, you are robbing God.

That is why the tithe is more than just a tithe. It is more than just a tenth. When a person gives ten percent of their income to God, what they are really doing is acknowledging that God owns the other ninety percent too! Ten percent is simply an acknowledgement and a confession that God owns it all.

The tithe is more than just that. The first part of our mission statement is that we are to love God. If you remember, I told you that one of the ways you love God is with your treasure. It is with your tithes and with your offerings. Just as God loved us and showed it to us by giving His Son, one of the ways we show God that we love Him is by giving Him His tithe.

Have you ever seen that bumper-sticker that says, "Honk if you love Jesus"? I saw one not long ago that I thought was a lot better than that. It said, "Tithe if you love Jesus. Anybody can blow their horn." That is the power of ten. It gives me the power to be in God's will and God's will is for me to be a giver and not a robber.

It Is The Power To Bless God's Work

In verse 10, Malachi gives the remedy for robbery. Let's break it down, part-by-part. First, he says, *"Bring the whole tithe"* (Mal. 3:10, NASB). Each word there is important. First of all, you are to bring it with you. Part of your worship to God is the financial offering that you bring to Him when you come to His house. You are not to bring a tip. You are to bring a tithe. Some people treat the offering the same way they treat the bill at a restaurant and they just simply give a tip.

I read the other day about a one-dollar bill that met up with a twenty-dollar bill. The one-dollar bill said, "Where have you been? I haven't seen you around very much." The twenty-dollar bill said, "I've been on the road. I have been everywhere. I have been hanging out at casinos, going on cruises, at the golf course, baseball games, out to the mall and I've been having a blast. How about you?" The dollar bill said, "Same old stuff. You know… church, church, church."

We are not to bring a tip to God. We are to bring the tithe to God – that is the first ten percent of what we earn. That includes every source of your income whether it is a paycheck, the sale of real estate, or stocks, or bonds, or dividends. Whatever is the source of income, the first ten percent belongs to God.

Then we are not only told what to bring, but where to bring it. We are to bring it *"to the storehouse."* The storehouse was a storage room in a temple where people would come and deposit their tithes and offerings. There is a modern day storehouse because the New Testament church is the counterpart to the Old Testament temple.

In 1 Corinthians 16:2 the apostle Paul said, "*On the first day of the week let each one of you lay something aside storing up as he may prosper that there be no collections when I come*" (1 Cor. 16:2, NKJV). Do you see the words there "*storing up?*" That is a play on words based on the concept of the storehouse in the Old Testament. Paul was simply saying to the New Testament church what they did in the Old Testament when they brought their tithes to the temple, you are to do today by bringing your tithes to the [local] church.

That is why the prophet Malachi is specific when he says, "*Bring your whole tithe to the storehouse*" (Mal. 3:10, NASB). There are some people who think they can give their tithe anywhere they want to give it. God has commanded us not only what to give. He has commanded us where to give it. There is nothing wrong with supporting other organizations and there is nothing wrong with supporting other charities and other people who do good things for God, but your tithe belongs to the [local] church. If you are not tithing to the church, you are really not tithing.

God was so specific about the tithe being brought to the place of worship, to His house, that He said in Deuteronomy 12:11, "*You must bring everything I command you – your burnt offerings, your sacrifices, your tithes, your sacred offerings, and your offerings to fulfill a vow – to the designated place of worship, the place, the Lord your God chooses for His name to be honored*" (Deut. 12:11, NLT). That obviously is the church (today).

Just as a footnote, you remember in verse 8 he talks about robbing God in tithes and offerings. The tithe is not a ceiling that you stop at, but a floor you stand on. The tithe is not the maximum. It is the minimum. Financially, tithing is the first grade of giving. You don't get to graduate school until you give an offering. What is the purpose of the tithe and the offering?

He goes on to say, "*So that there may be food in My house.*" That simply means that the tithe is God's way of financing the work of

His church. I want you to stop for a moment and think about what you learned and what happens when you finally decide to write out a check and give God His tithe for His work. Let me show you how the power of ten is unleashed in that magical moment. Think about all the powerful lessons you are taught when you give that tithe.

Think about, first of all, just writing the check out. The first thing you do when you write out a check you enter the date. Automatically, you are reminded that you are a creature of time. One of these days, you are going to die and leave it all behind and everything you have is either going to rust or burn, so the best thing you can do is give it while you can.

Then, you put down the name of whom you are writing the check to. I wish the bank would cash it. You could just write out the name "God," because that is actually who you are giving your money to, but since they don't do that you write out the name of the church which is simply God's representative.

When you write out the amount of the check, which is your tithe, and you realize you are giving it to God's work, you just made a confession. You just confessed that you understand that God owns everything you have anyway and it all belongs to Him.

Then, you know that line that is in the lower left-hand corner of the check where you write what the check is for? You could write down all kinds of things there. Yes, it is for paying light bills, and literature, and salaries, but it is also for marriages to be restored, for lives to be changed, for people to be saved, for teenagers to go on mission trips, for the dying and sick to be ministered to and prayed for, and for the Gospel to be preached. Even more, it pays for the way the church has blessed your family and blessed your marriage and serves ready to help you in any time of spiritual need that you might have. Yes, the tithe is the power to bless God's work and to bless you at the same time.

It Is The Power To Believe God's Word

A few years ago, you may remember that Pepsi created an ad campaign that they called, "The Pepsi Challenge." They asked consumers to compare their brand of fizz with that of their chief rival (and we all know who that is). They said, "We believe that our fizz tastes better than theirs and we are willing for you to try it and prove it." God does something in relation to the power of ten that He never does anywhere else in the Bible. He asks us to test it. He gives us the tithing challenge. He says, *"Test me now in this," says the Lord of hosts, "If I will not open for you the windows of heaven and pour out for you a blessing until it overflows"* (Mal. 3:10, NASB).

Now God beats us to the punch. He says, "I am willing to put My money where My mouth is." He says when we open up our wallet and give Him His tithe, He will open up His window and give us His blessing. Now, I want to cut to the chase. God just made a deal that you cannot refuse if you believe God.

If you take that verse at face value then there can only be one reason why a follower of Christ doesn't tithe – only one. Because, he doesn't believe God. He doesn't take God at His Word. Now, we are getting to where the rubber really hits the road. Tithing has nothing to do with your finances. It has everything to do with your faith. If you don't hear anything else I've said, I hope and pray you will believe this. Tithing is not God's way of getting something from you. It is God's way of giving something to you.

Here is the way it works. When you put God first in the area of your finances, God gets involved in your finances and God blesses it and God makes sure that you don't out give Him. Deuteronomy 14:23 says, "The purpose of tithing is to teach you to always put God first in your lives." Do you know what tithing does? It not only puts your money where it belongs, it puts God where He belongs.

Tithing is not a matter of what you think about giving. Tithing is a matter of what you think about God. Do you trust the person of God that He will keep His word? Do you trust the power of God to meet every financial need that you have? Do you trust the promise of God to honor you if you will honor Him? If the answer to those questions is, "Yes," you won't have to tithe, you will want to tithe. You not only will want to tithe, but you will also want to start giving an offering above.

On the basis of everything that we have listened to and read today, let me ask you this question. Are you giving to God what is right or what is left? Does your money come before God or does God come before your money?

8

Well Done to Those Who Have Done Well
Part 3 of "The Giver, the Getter and God" series
PHILIPPIANS 4:14-25 (KJV)
Johnny Hunt
President of 1996 Pastors' Conference

*"And my God shall supply all your needs according to His riches in
glory by Christ Jesus. Now, to our God and Father is glory forever
and ever. Amen. Greet every saint in Christ Jesus; the brethren who
are with me greet you. All the saints greet you but especially those
who are of Caesar's household. The grace of our Lord Jesus Christ
be with you all, Amen."*

– Philippians 4:19-25.

Previously, I introduced one major thought. I talked about Paul's
commendation for the Philippians' financial commitment.
The region of Macedonia, which is referenced in 2 Corinthians 8
and 9, was one of the most poverty stricken areas of the world. Yet
the Philippian Church, which is right in the middle of Macedonia,
made a sacrificial gift on more than one occasion and greatly
blessed Paul. So Paul writes and he says, "I want to thank God for
your gift."

Now here is a question: Why did he not say I want to thank *you*
for your gift? Well, he ultimately did thank them but he gave God
the credit because he felt that it was the Holy Spirit that prodded
their hearts to be obedient to give the gift. So Paul comes out with
a heart full of gratitude. He thanks them for being interested in his
need. They identified with his need and were involved in meeting
the need. He shared with the Philippians that of all the churches
in the world, of all the people he has influenced, the church at

Philippi for ten years had joined in helping him. If anybody had a worthy ministry for supporting, it would have been the Apostle Paul. But only that church had reached out to him.

So in verse 15 and 16 of chapter 4, he uses accounting terminology, giving and receiving. He just thanks them for giving out of their poverty to meet a need in his life.

Then I talked about the teachings of Jesus where in Luke 6:38 Jesus gave us a conditional promise. He said, "*Give and it will be given unto you, good measure, pressed down, shaken together, running over will be put into your bosom. For with the same measure that you use, it will be measured back to you.*" Look at this promise. I don't want to read anything into it. I just want to give you the pure Word of God. The Lord Jesus said, "*Give, and it will be given to you.*" If you believe that, say "Amen." I do too. Because He said so. Because the Bible says it.

It says God would give the same measure that He would give unto your bosom or translated in English vernacular, He would give unto your lack. That means that you would have to take your long-flowing gown and pull it up, to hold all that God blessed you with. And He said I will measure to you the same that you have measured to Me.

I will ask you a question: All I want to do is get our minds thinking in the right way. Is what you placed in the offering a moment ago, if God were to give you back with the same measure that you gave to Him, could you make it this week?

For instance, let's just use the tithe. If Jesus gave you ten times what you gave Him this morning, would you do all right next week? Or are some of you saying, "No, if He did that, I'd have to sing your favorite hymn, 'Help Me Rhonda'."

So, the bottom line is, He says, "I will give in the same measure." So here's what He's saying: "Giving is governed by receiving and

WELL DONE TO THOSE WHO HAVE DONE WELL

receiving is governed by giving."

Recently, I dealt with Paul's celebration of their spiritual consecration. He was celebrating the fact that the people in Philippi were set aside, dedicated their time and their treasures. They were totally devoted followers of Jesus Christ. Why did Paul celebrate their spiritual consecration?

First, because the church gave maturely to Paul and received spiritually from the Lord.

Secondly, because Paul's real joy was not what the gift did for him, but what the gift did for them. If you gave this morning, you may say, "I blessed the church." Yes, you did but not like God's going to bless you. You are the benefactor when you give, not the fellowship that receives it. We just receive your act of obedience.

Third, because no gift we make to God ever leaves us poor. If you've read my life story, you read about a fellow by the name of Otis Scruggs. He was a member of my first church in Gaffney, South Carolina at Livonia Baptist Church. Here's the truth he taught me. He said, "You'll never miss anything you give away." And I say, "To God be the glory, amen." Otis, thanks for teaching your pastor that.

Fourth, because it provided for his need, it also allows them to get in on the giving cycle of eternity.

Fifth, because he was happy for them because of what they would receive as a result of their giving. Paul said, "What you've given has actually been a profit or a fruit that has actually blessed you." That's what he says in verse 17, *"Not that I need your gift or seek the gift but I seek the fruit that abounds to your account."*

We're fortunate if we get saved, live faithful to God and live long enough to be able to get in on the fruit that God brings through our ministry. Look at the fruit of Paul's labor. Luke was the fruit of his labor, a great physician and writer. And Onesimus, the slave became fruit of his labor. So Paul celebrated that.

But let me tell you what else he celebrated. He celebrated their giving. Giving and spirituality are inseparably linked. Jesus said, "*Wherever a man's treasure is, there will his heart be also.*" So my heart needs to be in what I'm in. One of the reasons I preach with fervency and urgency and passion is because I believe what I'm preaching. I really do. This truth has gotten hold of my heart and I thank God for the Word of God.

Martin Luther said, "I've held many things in my hand and I've lost them all, but whatever I place in God's hands, I still possess." What a great word.

Now, I want to call your attention to two truths.

Number One: Paul's Explanation Concerning The Spiritual Condition

I'll teach you something about your Bible and I want you to try to prove me wrong. You will find this to be true. When you're reading your Bible and you realize there's over four thousand personal promises in your Bible, you will also find that most of the promises in the Bible are conditional promises. As a matter of fact He said, "*Give and it will be given unto you.*"

I've made promises to my children. When they were little things, it was hard to get them to do chores. I had two little girls and they couldn't do some things.

I used to make promises to the kids. I'd say, "Deanna, if you and Holly will clean your room, at the end of the week, I'll give you an allowance." You know what they heard? Allowance. So at the end of the week they would come and say, "Dad, pay up." And I'd say, "No, you didn't clean up." "Oh, but you said you'd give us…" "But no, it was conditional, I told you I'd give you a gift if you cleaned up."

We're the same way. We try to come and claim the promises of God without fulfilling the conditions of the Word of God. The greatest need in the church is not for us to know our Bibles better, but to obey the part of the Bible we know.

The real test this morning is not that you read through the Bible, but that you obey the Bible. Not that you hear another sermon, but you will obey the preaching of the Word of God. There's a great need for obedience to the Word of God.

So here's what Paul's saying in verse 19, "You met my need and God is going to meet your needs. You met one need that I had but my God will meet all of your needs."

My friend, Bruce Schmitt, doesn't have a salary right now. At this point they're trusting God. He has a few preaching opportunities. He's going to be a Mission Service Corp faith volunteer. His wife, Martha, asked him yesterday, "Bruce, we're moving into the new year. What are we going to do about giving?" This will bless you. He said, "Well, Martha, what do we need a month to live on?" She said, 'Well, we need x number of thousand dollars per month." And he said, "Well, write a tithe check for that amount and we're going to trust God for it." Most of you who have got it, won't give it. He doesn't even have it and he's going to trust God.

"*My God shall supply all your needs according to His riches in glory in Christ Jesus.*" Put Him to the test. I said, "Oh really?" Then I found out that Iris and Duane Blue are faith missionaries and do you know what they do? They give based on their needs. They usually say, "Our money is running a little short and next month we've got a lot of needs coming. We need to increase our giving."

Why am I telling you this? I'm telling you I'm excited about the truth of God's Word. Here's what Blue said, "You met one need that I had but my God will meet, my God shall supply, *all* your needs." Wait a minute. You mean they responded and sent about three or four offerings and God committed to meet all their needs?

That's exactly what He did.

Hudson Taylor said, "When God's work is done God's way for God's glory, it will not lack for God's supply." Wow! I believe one of the reasons God has supplied every single need at First Baptist, Woodstock is because we, the best we know how under the wisdom of God, have tried to do God's work in God's way, for God's glory and then there has been God's supply.

So you need to know that a lot of the Scripture promises are verses that you and I have no Scriptural right to whatsoever if we are not willing to obey its conditional truth. Some people erroneously take this verse out of its context and try to claim the promises without meeting the condition. But the principle in verse 18 must be acted upon first if the truth of verse 19 is to be enjoyed. Most of God's promises are conditional and most of us are ready and willing to accept the blessing but overlook the obligation.

If there's one word I say to the American church in the twenty-first century, it is that the cross is God's riches at Christ's expense. But it demands divine responsibility. I just get saved and nothing else matters. I'm in. No, my friend, God wants you to grow in the grace and divine knowledge of Jesus Christ.

Listen to this promise, now catch it, and don't miss it. Proverbs 3:9 says, "*Honor the Lord with your possessions and with the first fruit of all your increase so your barns will be filled with plenty and your vats will overflow with new wine.*" God is saying, "Honor Me first. Don't give Me your leftovers. Give Me your first possessions."

Here's what God said to the priests. When you bring an offering to Me, bring a spotless, unblemished lamb and let it be a male. Guess what the priest brought God? A blind, female lamb. The dude couldn't even see. And here's what they do. They take them down there to the high priest and they would check them out and they would look up there and say, "We're not going to accept this lamb." Do you know what I did last Sunday? I jumped off the platform, ran down and picked on one of the congregation and I played as though we were taking an offering in the Old Testament. In the Old Testament there would be someone that would examine your gift and if it was not the proper gift, they wouldn't accept it.

Could you imagine me doing that this morning? Going down there and watching you drop your envelope in the offering plate. Say I stood beside one of our stingy members who gave five dollars. "Five dollars, well you're supposed to give a tithe so that means you only made fifty dollars this week?" One of two things. He needs prayer or he needs repentance.

I stood beside John C. and I said, "John, we're not going to take that offering. Shame on you. You get out of here and come back with a worthy offering." Well, you can imagine what was happening in the pews behind him. They were getting nervous. We just don't realize what we have under grace. Thank God.

Somebody says, "Why do you preach tithing? Isn't that an Old Testament principle?" Yes sir, it is. It was four hundred years before the law and Jesus commended it in Matthew 23:23. Let me go a step further. This is my personal conviction. You don't have to buy into it. I am not trying to push it off on you. I confess I need discipline and organization in my life. I don't need to fly by the seat of the pants. I don't need to say, "Well, sometime this week I'm going to try to prepare a sermon for next week." No. Early in the morning I get alone with God down in my study and I begin to pray and labor over the Word of God. Then I spend hours in the study laboring over God's Word so I will have something to say. It may not be what you want to hear but I've got something to say when I come on Sunday.

What if I just said, "I don't know what I'm going to give. I'll just give whatever comes to mind and I'll give a portion out of the proportion that God has given me." I'll guarantee the person that does this hardly gives anything.

Here's my conviction: If those Pharisees, under the demands of a righteous law, gave ten percent, God forbid that I do less than those jokers! Especially since I am now under the unmerited favor of God now that Jesus has manifested Himself on the cross on my behalf. Man, I want to do at least what they did. So for years, I've been doing at least and far more than what the Pharisees did. That's a good place to start. You can't out give God.

The promise is to encourage those who were sacrificial in their response to the needs of God's work. Here's what He's saying to me today. "You know, Bessie has some needs." That's my mom, Bessie Mae. And I'd say, "Yes, God has blessed me and I'm going to try to help momma." I love helping my momma. I tell my wife sometimes I wish she was still alive so I could just bless her. She blessed me so much.

But anyway, here's what happened. Robert tried to corner me one day. I was a new believer and he said, "Hey, you tithe over there at that church?" I said, "Yes sir, Robert, that's what the Bible teaches and yes sir, I give ten percent of my income to the Lord every week. Before I was a preacher, I tithed." Robert said, "Well, let me ask you something Brother Johnny. If your momma needed that money, wouldn't you just take that money and give it to her instead of giving it to the church and to God?" I said, "Nope." He said, "You wouldn't?" I said, "It ain't mine to give her. It's God's, it's holy unto the Lord. It ain't mine."

He said, "You mean you'd let her have that need?" I said, "Oh no. God promised me that if I would give, He would cause all grace to abound towards me so that I could be involved in every good work." And I said, "I want to tell you something: God is so involved when momma has a need that I don't have to choose between the two. My God is able to supply all of my needs according to His riches in glory in Christ Jesus. Not part of it, not just mine and my momma's. All our needs."

When momma needed some medicine or wanted me to pick her up some milk or bread, I always had the money to take care of her. Why? When God is in our hearts, His heart of compassion is prompting us to get involved in helping others. He is in our acts of generosity. When He is in our strong commitment and He's using our sacrifices to bless others, He does not forget us.

There's a couple here that joined our church last week. On a Sunday before they even became members of our church, they heard someone say that there was a missionary here that needed prayer because they needed to find a place to live. This couple intervened and made it possible for them to have a home. I'm almost embarrassed to say, but they sold this home for tens and tens of thousands of dollars less than what the house should have sold for. It is a beautiful house.

I believe that what this couple did is commendable. You see, the whole subject of finances and fund raising and remaining pure and humble and grateful and the handling of money is a heavy weight hanging on the thin, twin wires of integrity and accountability.

What is this promise of claim?

Number one: This promise is personal. A personal relationship. Verse 19 says, "*My God shall supply.*" The promise is personal.

Number two: The promise is positive. That word "supply" means to fill up something that's empty. In 2 Corinthians 9 we see that when the Philippians gave, believe me, there wasn't anything left. And God said, "*I'm going to fill up your emptiness.*" And He did. So it's positive.

Number three: The promise is pointed. He didn't just say, "Well, I'll bless you in some way or another." Here's what he said. "*My God shall supply all of your need.*" He pointed right there at the need.

God knows what your need is. Some of you sometimes think, "I'd better hold onto this, a cloudy day may come." Who's in charge of the weather for heaven's sakes? That's a promises principle. The Bible says, "*My God shall supply all your needs according to His riches in glory.*" It does not say *out* of His riches but *according* to His riches. If He took it out of something He had, there would be less left after He took it out. "According to" means it is limitless, inexhaustible. It means that even after all God has given me in the last twenty-seven years that I've been a child of God, He still has as much as He had to start with. Wow, I don't have anybody else in the world like that.

I watched Bill Gates on television with Larry King Live last night. He has eighty-five billion dollars. But every time he gives a billion away he has a billion less. Every time God gives something away, He's still got the same. Man, what a God! That's why we ought to read our Bibles to know more about God so we can praise Him better.

Number four: The promise is powerful. It says, "*In Jesus Christ.*" Listen to this. Lend your boat for a whole afternoon to Jesus Christ that it may be His floating pulpit and when He returns it to you it will be laden with fish. Place your upper room at his disposal for a single meal and He will fill your whole house with the Holy Ghost. Place in His hand your barley loaves and fish and He will not only satisfy your hunger, but will give you twelve baskets full.

Paul's confidence about God meeting the needs of others was directly relating to their being good stewards of what God entrusted to them. There's no license here for being irresponsible in financial affairs and yet thinking that God is obligated to meet a person's need just because he's a Christian. There are a lot of Christians that are in trouble financially because they've not met the condition of the promise.

What comprises God's riches? Psalm 50:10 says, "*For every beast of the field is mine and the cattle on a thousand hills."* Psalm 50:12 says, *"If I were hungry, I wouldn't tell you for the world is mine and its fullness."* But my favorite verse in the Bible about God taking care of us is Psalm 37:25. It says, *"I've been young and now am old yet I've not seen the righteous forsaken nor his seed beg bread."* Wow.

I've been young and now I'm older. I'm not old but I'm older. In my oldness, I've never begged bread. I've never been forsaken by the Righteous One. Have any of you known Him since you were young and now you're older and He's been faithful to you? Can I see that hand? Let's testify to Him. He is faithful.

Number Two: Paul's Salutation To Relational Conversion

He commenced with the doxology. Look at verse 20. Paul said this, *"My God shall supply all your needs according to His riches in glory in Christ Jesus."* Then he says in verse 21, *"Now to the God and Father be glory forever and ever amen."* That is a doxology. The word 'glory' is where we get our word for praising God. Praise God from whom all blessings flow. Praise Him above ye heavenly hosts. Praise Father, Son, and Holy Ghost.

Why do we sing a doxology? Why do people praise the Lord? Say you're sitting in a church and the church is dead and you're just sitting there and you shout, "Oh Glory!" Let me tell you, something is swelling up. You can hardly stand it anymore and then in a moment you erupt in praise.

Paul is sitting there and he's got that chain and he's dragging across the desk and he's writing this letter. He says, *"My God shall supply all your needs,"* and then he gets to thinking, *"all of them according to His riches, not out of, but according to His riches in glory by Christ Jesus."* And then he breaks out into doxology, "Oh glory to God." That's what he did in verse 20. He breaks into a doxology. He begins to sing it to God.

I read a statement this weekend that really blessed me. You preachers will enjoy this. Listen to this. "Doctrine is never a dry matter. Whenever it occupies his mind it also fills his heart with praise." I could be preaching this message this morning and be as dry as dust. I've known preachers that were so dry they couldn't spit. And you wonder why the people are so dry.

You let a great doctrine from the Word of God get hold of your heart and let it burn there and dwell. I came to church this morning and one verse was in my mind. *"I was glad when they said unto me, let us go into the house of the Lord."* Let me go a step further. He not only commits with doxology, he continued with salutation, he greets three groups of people. He says, *"Every saint in Christ Jesus."* Greet every saint in Christ Jesus.

I had lunch with a wonderful family here in our church and we were together over in Gatlinburg. I was speaking to thousands of teenagers and so they said, "Can we take you to lunch? Today we get to talk to you one-on-one." They asked, "Is it scary being the pastor of such a big church?" And I said, "No, it probably would be if I would have come here and the church was this big. But since I came here and it was small, I've grown with this church. It's kind of like buying a small house and adding rooms to it. You feel more familiar with it. You don't feel out of place. I really feel at home at Woodstock and I love everybody." The husband said, "You can't possibly know everybody, can you?" I said, "No, not now."

Then God put something on my heart I've never thought of. "I don't know all of you now. I know a whole bunch of you but I don't know all of you. But if you belong to Jesus, one day I will." I'm going to get to know all of you in heaven. I'm going to go ahead and make a commitment that for the first million years I'm going to hang out with this church family if the Lord will let me. Okay? Now if you're not going to be there, I can't make any promises to you. You're going to have to try to get to me in the next few years. Do you know what I mean? If you're saved and you know it, we will spend time together.

You may say, "Why did you say that, preacher?" Paul said, in a letter that's inspired by the Holy Ghost, "*I greet every saint.*" Here's what a Greek commentator said: Instead of using the collective 'all', Paul used the individualistic 'every' to declare that each saint was worthy of his concern. He didn't say, "I love all of you." He said, "I love every one of you."

What he's saying is every one of you is an individual that I love. I call the Holy Ghost as my witness –I love every one of you.

Well... I love you in the same way Paul loved everybody. And by the way, he told the church at Colossae he loved them and he had never been there. Why? Because the love of God was shed upon his heart by the Holy Ghost which was given unto him.

Let me go a step further. He's referring to saints. This did not say the brethren who are *for* me. He said the ones who are *with* me. There are a lot of people at Woodstock that are for me but they aren't with me. They're for Jesus, they're just not with Jesus. So, he said "*the brethren who are with me.*" I don't have time to explain who all those brothers are or who I think they are.

Let me show you last of all Caesar's household. Do you want to see fruits for your labor? Have you lived long enough to see your labors bear fruit for God? When the Bible says Caesar's household, it was probably a significant number of people. It didn't just say Caesar and his guards. His household. It was not limited to Caesar's family. Who does that include? Scholars believe that includes princes, couriers, judges, cooks, food tasters, musicians, custodians, builders, stablemen, soldiers, and accountants. I believe many people got saved under Paul's ministry, which was providential.

God put him in jail. He didn't just go to jail, God sent him to jail. It's like Monopoly. God said, "Go to jail and I'm not going to give you the free card to get out until you've done what I providentially placed you there to do." By being in jail he got to witness to some people he would have never witnessed to had he not been in jail.

You know what I believe happened? There are two guys cooking on a charcoal grill. "Hey, you off this afternoon?" "Yeah." "What you going to do?" "Ah…well, don't make fun of me but have you heard that man, Paul the Apostle?" "Yeah, man, I hear that everybody who goes over there has their lives change forever." "Go by and see him this afternoon. Two of my friends have been saved." And then the Bible records, *"and Caesar's household."*

The passage climaxed with a benediction. Last of all he says, *"The grace of our Lord Jesus be with you all."* If you'll study your Bible, you will find that Philippians 1:2 says, *"Grace and peace."* You can't have peace until you know the grace of God. It started in grace, it ended in grace.

Let me tell you what that was. *It was a reminder to all the people that Paul wrote to that he was condemned under sin.* Until he allowed the marvelous grace of God to come into his life for a personal relationship with Jesus Christ, he couldn't brag on grace. Ladies and gentlemen, listen to me, it ain't about church membership. It ain't about being a Baptist. It's about having the unmerited favor of God through Jesus Christ, a personal relationship with Him. That's what life is all about.

9

The Basics on Money Management
MATTHEW 6:24, 33-34 (NASB)
Bryant Wright
President of 2006 Pastors' Conference

There are basic things in Christian growth – like prayer, Bible study, and attending a church – that allow us opportunities to worship and experience Christian fellowship and serve the Lord. There's also the teaching in Christian growth about learning to share your faith, which is an important aspect of Christian growth. But it's interesting to me that so often in a focus on basic Christianity or on basic Christian growth there's a very important aspect of Jesus' teaching that is left out–money management.

The reality is that Jesus Christ speaks a great deal about money management all through Scripture. His teachings during His ministry on earth stressed how vitally important money management is in our relationship with God.

I want us to look at three verses from the Sermon on the Mount. There are 100+ verses in the Sermon on the Mount, and 25 of them (almost a fourth) deal with money and possessions. This was obviously an important topic to Jesus. Let's look Matthew 6:24 and 33-34. In these verses, Jesus says, "*No one can serve two masters; for either he will hate the one and love the other, or he will hold to one and despise the other. You can not serve God and man…But seek first His kingdom and His righteousness; and all these things shall be added to you. Therefore do not be anxious about tomorrow; for tomorrow will take care of itself. Each day has enough trouble of its own.*"

By mid-January, you have received most of the Christmas bills. It's a time when many of you are feeling a bit poorer. Some of you are looking at your bank statement or the bills in hand and are seeing some excessive debt over the next couple of months. On top of that, with a down market a lot of you are feeling even poorer. Chances are, there is insight you would like to learn today about money management. Chances are, the last person you'd ever think would talk to you about money management would be a preacher. The reality is that even though I have nothing of significance to say, Jesus Christ has a great deal to say about money management.

Why are we so hesitant to talk about this in the life of the church since is it so vitally important to our Christian growth? I think there are several reasons. Pastors often hesitate to talk about this because they know it's one of the main reasons people don't come to church. "The church is always talking about money. They're always asking for money." Whenever you see surveys about why people don't come to church, this is near the top of the list. Another reason pastors are hesitant is they realize the majority of those in the church who profess Christ are disobedient to the Lord in this area. Very often when biblical study is involved in this area, those people tend to squawk the loudest.

But there are also other reasons. Some people feel like money is a worldly thing, and in church we focus on spiritual things, and the two do not belong together. This is the exact opposite of what Jesus teaches. There's also a misguided understanding in that many believe they're quoting Scripture when they say, "Money is the root of all evil." That's not in the Bible. God's Word says, "*The **love** of money is the root of all **sorts** of evil*," a very different matter indeed.

This morning we want to look to God's Word, specifically to the words of Jesus Christ, and we want to begin to understand the basics of money management and how to apply God's Word to our everyday lives.

Look with me, first of all, at the words of Jesus in Matthew 6:24. "*No one can serve two masters. Either he will hate the one and love the other or he will hold to one and despise the other. You can not serve*

God and man [or God and materialism or God and money]." Some of you are thinking to yourselves, "Jesus was probably wrong about that. I want to serve both." No, Jesus is saying you've got to make a choice. What He is telling us right out of the shoot is that the first basic step in money management is to make a choice. You've got to make a big decision. Is it going to be God or is it going to be money?

Some of you are still confused. You're saying, "Why do I have to choose between the two?" Jesus Christ understands that the big decision is about ownership. Who is going to be the owner of our lives, the Lord of our lives, the master of our lives? Jesus is saying you can't serve two masters. A slave or a servant cannot serve two masters. They've got to serve one. Unless you and I choose God and give God the ownership of our lives and put our trust in God, we're going to put our trust in our bank accounts, in our financial portfolios, in our money, in what we earn.

It's just the reality of life because Jesus knows that for most of us the big competition for lordship of our lives has to do with our money and possessions. The reality is that money can be a very demanding slave master. Let me read you an interesting quote from Bill Hybels in his book, *Honest to God?*.

> It beckons and woos us. It tantalizes and seduces us. It sucks us into its grasp and wreaks havoc in our lives. And still we deny its sinister power. A Money Monster? Ha! There's no such thing...Meanwhile, we devote our lives to earning it, glory in spending it, and lie awake nights figuring out how to stockpile more of it. We pursue inauthentic jobs because of it. We bow at its feet and salute its command. There's a Money Monster all right, sly and artful. He's been around for centuries, but during the last twenty years he's moved from the shadows into the mainstream of American life.

That's very interesting insight in thinking about how dominant our thoughts, our orientation about money can be. When people tell me that money means nothing to them I often chuckle and say, "Well give it all away if it means nothing to you." That would be stupid because money is very important not only to all of us in our orientation in life, but it's also very important to God. What Jesus is telling us is we've got to make a decision.

Think about it this way. Why is it that the number one excuse people give when asked about why they are not interested in Christianity is because the church is always talking about money? Certainly, the outrageousness of some TV evangelists is part of the reason. However, the bottom line is what Jesus is explaining. The reason people say that is because they are screaming volumes about what their master is, where their faith is. What they're really saying is, "Ain't nobody going to mess with my money, not even the church." The reality is about enslavement – who is your Lord, who is the owner of your life, what is the priority of your life? That's really the decision that Jesus calls on us to make.

Some of you say you've chosen God. I have a question for you: How do you know you've chosen God? When it comes to money management, when it comes to possessions, how do you know? Matthew 6:33 begins to reveal some understanding as Jesus continues to teach about money and possessions. Look at what He says: "*Seek first His kingdom and His righteousness and all these things will be added to you.*" The starting point of understanding, if we have truly given our hearts and given ownership of our lives and given our trust to God, lies in seeking first His kingdom business.

Whenever we have a priority in our lives, we are going to invest in it. Jesus is saying if money is a priority, your checkbook is going to reveal it very quickly because your checkbook is not going to lie about where you're investing your funds. But if God is your priority, then preeminent in your priority list is going to be the investment in Kingdom business. What does your bank account, your investments, your checkbook say about your attitudes toward God and money?

Jesus goes on. In Matthew 6:19 He says, "*Do not lay for yourself treasures upon earth where moth and rust destroy, where thieves break in and steal. But, lay up for yourselves treasures in heaven where neither moth nor rust destroys where thieves do not break in and steal, for where your treasure is there your heart will be.*" Jesus is saying that wherever you invest, wherever you write those checks, wherever you spend that money – that is where your heart is. You're revealing your heart.

Question: What does your checkbook or your bank account say about your heart for God? Jesus is making it so clear to us here. Do you really believe in heavenly matters? Do you really believe in Kingdom business, enough to invest in it? Or is your whole orientation wrapped up in the things of this world – in things that can rust, that moths can get a hold of, that after a while become useless to you if you tend to hoard what you have?

Jesus is saying, "I want you to invest in a risk-free investment with eternal return because investment in Kingdom business, a Christ-centered ministry, is an investment in people." When you invest in a Christ-centered church, a Christ-centered ministry, you're investing in Kingdom business. The treasure that Jesus talks about is those lives that come to Jesus Christ because of your investment in Kingdom business through your time, your talents, and your financial resources. That is how you build up heavenly treasure.

Jesus is saying, "Look, I want to talk to you about investments. I want you to invest in a risk-free investment that has lasting returns." You're going to enjoy these returns in heaven as you come across people whose lives have been touched, who have come to Christ for salvation because you invested in Kingdom business. That's a lasting investment that Jesus wants us to be conscious of. Otherwise, we tend to hoard what we have. After a while, even that becomes useless when it doesn't work anymore, when we can't wear it anymore, or it's of no good to us.

He gives a vivid contrast. So then the question arises, "How can I be right with God in this area?" Look back at Matthew 6:33. Jesus says, *"Seek first His kingdom and His righteousness."* How do you begin to be right when it comes to money management, when it comes to investing in heavenly treasures?

Turn to Proverbs 3. Listen to what the Word of God says in verses 9 and 10; *"Honor the Lord from your wealth and from the first of all your produce so that your barns may be filled with plenty and your vats will overflow with new wine."* The starting point is to honor God with our first fruits. In other words, when we earn money we're to give to the Lord first of all and not last. We're to give to Him our best and not just what is left over. That is the starting point.

But the question arises, "How much do I give?" The Bible has given clear guidance. God calls on us to give a tithe. A tithe is 10% of what we earn, the first fruits of the Lord. This is not just Old Testament law, as a lot of misguided Christians may feel. If you look in Genesis 14, Abraham, hundreds of years before the giving of the law, gave a tithe to Melchizedek, the high priest. It was a way of acknowledging gratitude to God for what God had done. You read in the New Testament in the teachings of Jesus Christ in Matthew 23:23 that Jesus upholds the importance of the tithe as the starting point. It is not the arrival point or the working up to something. It's the starting point in faithful giving.

Some of you are saying, "Well I can't give 10%." You think about the income that you achieved and you think you can't give 10% with all the obligations you have. You are right, you can't – at least not on your own. It takes the life-changing power of Christ to develop that kind of faith and trust in God – to develop the kind of unselfishness that is willing to trust God and recognize that He has entitled you to be a manager of the 90% that He allows you to keep. If we do not do that, the Scripture is very clear that we are robbing God because the tithe is kind of like an owner's fee. If we have literally given our lives to God, then He says, "OK, here's the owner's fee, here's the starting point, the tithe. This is the way you acknowledge that I am the owner of your life." This is the way you live righteously with God. And if we don't, we're robbing God.

In the early days of Johnson Ferry, in the mid-80s, some thieves broke into the church one Sunday afternoon and stole the safe. They literally took it out and hauled it off. All of the Sunday offering was in it. For the next couple of weeks, people around the church were just appalled. How in the world could anybody stoop so low as to rob a church? There are lots of folks who profess Christ that stoop even lower every Sunday as they continue to rob God. It is much worse to rob God than to rob the church. Those crooks probably don't know God, but there are a lot of people in the church that profess Christ, and yet they rob God weekly.

Some of you may think that's a little harsh. Let's look at the Word of God. Turn to the last book of the Old Covenant. In Malachi 3:8-10, the prophet Malachi is speaking to people of faith. Listen to the Word of God: "*Will a man rob God? Yet you are robbing Me, and you say, 'How have we robbed Thee?' And God says, 'in tithes and contributions.' You're cursed with a curse for you are robbing me the whole nation of you. Bring the whole tithe into the storehouse so that there may be food in My house and test Me now in this, as the Lord of Hosts, if I will not open for you the windows of heaven and pour out to you a blessing until there is no more need.*" I hope you've begun to pick up on what is happening in Scripture after Scripture, whether it's the Proverbs passage about first fruits, the Malachi passage about bringing the whole tithe into the storehouse which is their place of worship, or whether it's the teaching of Jesus on the Sermon on the Mount.

Turn back to our text for today. In Matthew 6:33, in the third part of that verse, look at what it says, "*Seek first His kingdom [that's the starting point] and His righteousness [in other words, we want to invest righteously] and all these things shall be added unto you.*" You see the theme that Scripture is teaching, that God's Word is teaching over and over. You trust Me, you put Me first, you live righteously with Me in money management, and all these things, all these needs, will be added to you.

That leads to another major question: Do you trust God? What does your checkbook and your bank account say about your trust? Do you trust in your bank account, in your financial portfolio, in what you earn? Or do you trust in God? What does it say? The checkbook doesn't lie.

Scripture goes on in Matthew 6:34. *"Therefore don't be anxious for tomorrow for tomorrow will take care of itself. Each day has enough trouble of its own."* It's very interesting to me that in the context of this whole section where Jesus is talking about money and money management, He gives a very interesting analogy. Look back at verse 25: *"For this reason, I say to you do not be anxious for your life as to what you shall eat or what you shall drink nor for your body as to what you shall put on. Is not life more than food and the body more than clothing?"* Now listen to what He says. *"Look at the birds of the air, they don't sow, neither do they reap or gather into the barns, and yet your heavenly Father feeds them."*

And listen to what He adds. *"Are you not worth much more than they?"* There is no doubt that God has created man in His image to be the most important creation of God, and Jesus Christ comes along and says, "There's no need for you to be anxious. Instead, you want to learn from the birds. They go about working from dawn to dusk, and God provides for them. They are not worried about tomorrow. Learn from them."

What is the message to all of us? Put our trust in God, seek first His kingdom and His righteousness, trust the promises of God. It's also a reminder to work hard. The idea of trusting God doesn't mean we sit back and say, "OK, God bless me, provide me with all that I need." No, we learn from the birds. We start with trust and then we work hard day in and day out, keeping our focus on

God rather than being overwhelmed with worries and anxieties and fears of tomorrow.

In that regard, I have a confession to you. I shared this confession with the elders in the latter part of 1999. In the spring of '99, a lot of us were led to make a pledge to our "God Can" building campaign for the facility that opened last August. As God dealt with Anne and me concerning that, we were led to make a pledge over the 3-year period that was double what we had given in any campaign before.

My family and I were doing that in the midst of our "mal-tuition" years of paying out-of-state tuition on two of our sons. It was a tough decision, but we really felt led by the Lord and had a peace about it. However, in the months that followed I began to start waking up at night trying to figure out how to pay for college, contemplating all we had saved for college and afraid that what we'd saved was going to run out very quickly as a result of making this pledge for "God Can." I was afraid that not only would we be unable to pay for college, but we would not be able to meet that pledge, as well.

As I was struggling with this, I began to get aggravated with myself. After all, I'm the pastor of the church. God has blessed time and time again. Why should I be so uptight? I was aggravated and embarrassed with myself. Why couldn't I trust? It was as if I was listening to the words of the devil as he whispered in my ear. I had said to people time and time again, "There's a fine line between foolishness and faith." It's like the devil was saying, "Hey boy, you've stepped over that line this time."

I was filled with anxiety about tomorrow as I looked at what we had saved for college and at what we had pledged. I asked the elders to pray with me because I realized my problem was trust and I had to confess to God that I needed His power, His Holy Spirit, to give me the power to trust Him. When we focus on the bank account, on the demands of tomorrow, we tend to be fearful and anxious and afraid. This is especially true when the economy doesn't look as rosy as it has looked for so many years. That's human nature. We need to confess to God, "Lord, help me trust in that area."

The Lord began to restore my peace by taking me back to Matthew 6:33 and 34 during my quiet times. He was telling me, "Trust Me. Trust Me. Trust Me. Keep your eyes on Me. Trust Me." That trust began to grow again and that inner peace began to come and the anxiety began to depart.

Now, here we are a little over half way through the "God Can" commitment. Our boys are still in college and we've been able to pay for that and keep up with our "God Can" commitment right on schedule. It's just a reminder of the promise of God to seek first His kingdom and His righteousness and all these things shall be added unto you.

The question I have for you today is this: are you willing to truly trust God in this area? If you are, then it begins with a decision of ownership. God or possessions. God or money. It also begins with a decision to invest in His kingdom and Kingdom business according to the teaching of the Scriptures and then trusting Him to meet your needs. That's the decision. If you're willing to make that decision, let me suggest to you some very practical aspects of money management. This is really a combination, if you will, of years of studying the Scripture as well as practical principles in money management that could perhaps be of help to you and your faith walk.

Spend less than you earn. Shocking isn't it? What a revelation. Very simple. Spend less than you earn. How do you do that? You need to have a budget because until you know what you earn, know what your financial obligations are, know what you're spending, what your wealth is, what your financial portfolio says then it's really hard to be sure that you're spending less than you earn. It's hard to be sure that you're being a good money manager. You need that basic information.

Realize that we are stewards. We have a responsibility to make the most of the resources that God has given us. When we understand this, then we begin to realize that every spending decision is just as spiritual as every giving decision. It's all about the management of God's funds. That's how God wants us to understand it.

But hear this concerning your budget, especially men. Men, that budget is not a legal document; it is not a written contract that your wife can never break. It is a goal, a plan, to help you be a good steward of what God has entrusted to you. A budget can be changed.

Give to God first. What do you have in that budget? You begin with giving. Remember the first fruits and the concept of giving off the top. How do you give righteously? It begins with a tithe. Some of you are going to be led by the Holy Spirit to give an offering over and above the tithe to certain ministries that God has put on your heart. Some of you are going to be led to give to certain charities or to family members or to education matters, etc. But, it begins by giving to the Lord. Then you develop giving to the categories in your budget. You have a game plan of what you are going to do, of what God is leading you to do.

Savings and investments. I've found in my own life that an automatic withdrawal from the checking account is the best-forced discipline in savings and investments. You can develop whatever the best forced discipline is for you. When it comes to savings, it's always good to remember that, as a Christian, you need to know why you are saving. Certainly there's the teaching of the ants in Proverbs 6. But we need to also consider the reason behind saving.

In other words, there will be long-term savings decisions and short-term savings decisions. What do we mean by that? A long-term savings decision could be saving for college or saving for retirement. In the last couple of years, we have actually spent more than we have earned because of our sons' out-of-state college tuition. However, we've been able to pay for it without debt because of all those years of savings and investments. That was a long-term savings goal.

There are also short-term savings goal such as vacations, Christmas, and unexpected expenses that come along. All of that is part of good financial planning, but there needs to be a reason behind the savings. Otherwise, after a while it will be the prideful mindset of building that financial portfolio just to know we have it. That's not what it's all about.

Taxes. Scripture is very clear; we are to pay what we owe. The teaching of Jesus in Matthew 22 says, "*Give unto Caesar what is Caesar's; give unto God what is God's.*" You also see this taught in Romans 13:6-7. We're to pay our taxes in order to underwrite the cost of government.

The question often comes up, "How can I lower my taxes?" The first way is to make less money. Most people tend to ignore that. The second way is to elect officials that will lower your taxes. You have that freedom in democracy. Let me give you an example of that in Commissioner Burns' State of the County address recorded in *The Atlanta Journal-Constitution*: "House Bill 1166 passed through the General Assembly, signed by the governor, and approved by the taxpayers and voters of Cobb County is permanent property tax relief. What that basically does is (as of January 1 of this year) address the issue of taxation, property taxes and reassessment. Number 1: in the future, reassessment of your residential properties will be a function of determining value, not taxation, because your property taxes for government services are frozen as long as you live in the home you're in." That's a new law that's been passed by government officials that we have elected. "Secondly, the best kept secret in this town is that at age 62, each and every one of you as property owners in this county will no longer be required to pay taxes for education. That's a 67% reduction in your property taxes." Now that's dramatic. Some of you that have just reached that age are saying, "I didn't know that. Good news." After 40-something years of supporting the public education system, the government says you've paid your dues. That's one example of government officials taking tangible steps to lower taxes.

So, making less money is not the only way you can lower your taxes. You can elect government officials that desire to lower taxes. With that in mind, I encourage you to pray for our president and the Congress. If you'll begin to calculate out how much you are spending as a result of government taxation through federal income tax, state income tax, social security, property tax, and taxes for dying and being married, you'll begin to see what an extraordinarily large amount of your income that is. But never forget, we must pay what we owe the government.

Fixed expenses. In your budget, you want to clearly know what your fixed expenses are. Some examples are: mortgage or rent, car payments, monthly groceries, utilities, etc. These are expenses we can't decide to skip a month or two.

Discretionary spending. This is an area that a lot of people tend to be the most interested in. What is discretionary spending? It is spending money on things that are important but not necessary at the time such as clothing, furniture, vacations or entertainment.

The question arises, "How do I wisely manage discretionary spending?" The preferred way in most homes is to eliminate your credit card debt. Then, "How can I increase the amount available for discretionary spending?" The first way is to make the decision to reduce your fixed expenses in order to increase your discretionary spending. The second way is to increase your income.

Understanding these basic principles and putting them into

action should be motivated by the Lordship of Jesus Christ. Remember that if you profess to be a Christian, you shouldn't be managing your money for yourself or your family as much as you should be for the Lord.

That means that a lot of you, in order to continue to grow spiritually, need to clear this hurdle of being a faithful money manager in God's eyes. I really believe the two biggest hurdles for new Christians and long-time Christians are to learn how to share your faith personally and manage your money in a way that glorifies Christ.

I want to encourage you today. Choose God or money. If you think it is not actually necessary to have to choose between the two then recognize this. If you don't choose God, your money will choose you, and it becomes a demanding slave master.

It's about ownership. Does God really own your life or does your money? Where are your trust and security? Are they in your bank account and in your investments or in God?

I encourage you to put your trust in God; to seek His kingdom business in everything. To do so is a risk-free investment that has eternal returns. Do this righteously by giving in a way that is pleasing to the Lord as prescribed by scripture.

Remember, it's all about trust. Do you believe the promise of God that He will meet our needs as we learn to be faithful to Him in this area? He will meet our needs. He says it in the Old Covenant and He says it in the New.

The choice is yours. What have you chosen? What will you choose – God or money? Jesus and His kingdom or anxiety, worry and fear about tomorrow? I encourage you, choose God and begin to experience the thrill and the joy of growing as a Christian in this vitally important area. God, in His Word, gives you the key to the basics of good money management.

10

Out On a Limb
LUKE 19:1-10 (NASB)
Hayes Wicker
President of 2007 Pastors' Conference

Jesus loves the lost, the last, the least, the little, and the losers. He even picked an M.D.P. (Most Despised Person) for His team. Zaccheus was a sell-out tax collector who collaborated with the occupying Romans. He was called a publican. One little boy, trying to explain his Sunday School lesson to his mother, said, "Jesus ate with the Republicans and sinners" (He must have been a Democrat). But Zaccheus was a "publican" and the head of the whole mafia-like cartel in Jericho, one of the three leading cities in Israel.

Many of you only know this guy from the children's song; "*Zaccheus was a wee little man.*" He was physically short, vertically challenged. When my daughter, Kristin, was a little girl, her favorite part was, "Zaccheus, you come down!" But I don't think that Jesus had a scolding tone and shook His finger like little Kristin did. He had open arms.

Everybody has a network. Zaccheus probably heard of how Levi (called Matthew) was following Jesus and that this unusual Teacher was "a friend of tax collectors and sinners." He heard that He was passing through town, but the crowd with their sharp elbows boxed out Zaccheus. It was only by climbing into one of those 40-feet high trees with a short trunk and wide branches that he could see Jesus. He was hoping to be camouflaged among the leaves, not be embarrassed as a seeker trying to check out this Christ.

The great Baptist preacher, Vance Havner, used to say, "Many are so afraid of getting out on a limb with God that they never get up the tree." New Age guru, Shirley MacClaine, described herself as "being out on a limb." A Christian wrote a book rebuking her occultic views, called "Out on a Broken Limb." God wants us, in faith, to get up the tree and out on a limb for Him, particularly in the area of giving, thus finding God's fruit.

Then Jesus entered and passed through Jericho. Now behold, there was a man named Zacchaeus who was a chief tax collector, and he was rich. And he sought to see who Jesus was, but could not because of the crowd, for he was of short stature. So he ran ahead and climbed up into a sycamore tree to see Him, for He was going to pass that way. And when Jesus came to the place, He looked up and saw him, and said to him, "Zacchaeus, make haste and come down, for today I must stay at your house." So he made haste and came down, and received Him joyfully. But when they saw it, they all complained, saying, "He has gone to be a guest with a man who is a sinner." Then Zacchaeus stood and said to the Lord, "Look, Lord, I give half of my goods to the poor; and if I have taken anything from anyone by false accusation, I restore fourfold." And Jesus said to him, "Today salvation has come to this house, because he also is a son of Abraham; for the Son of Man has come to seek and to save that which was lost."

Everyone Is Out On Some Kind Of Broken Limb

People are out on the broken limb of lostness (verse 10)

Jesus concluded this incident with the statement that He came to *seek and to save that which was lost.* That summarizes His whole ministry. Whether you trust in New Age thought or just old-fashioned works-based religion, your limb is fatally flawed.

Some change the name of their church, because they are apparently embarrassed by the term "church." They may call themselves a "center" or a "fellowship." Some have even called a church building, a "cultural center." But we are a church, a soul-saving lighthouse in the midst of a storm. Like Zaccheus, everyone needs Jesus, His salvation, and His people. We are the "called out ones" – called from lostness into life.

People are also out on the broken limb of deceit (verse 8)

Zaccheus later mentioned "defrauding" people, a perk of his position. He would charge any amount that he could get away with in taxes. Many Americans are also deceitful. In the 1990's, 59.4% of Americans indicated that they had called in sick to get a day off though they were well. Actually, all hearts are "deceitful above all things" (Jer. 17:9). That word for "deceit" had the original meaning of swelling up like a knoll or tripping up the heels. Our pride is a trap!

A mom caught her little boy "fibbing," a sugarcoated word for lying: "I thought you told me you had a lesson in church about honesty. What does the Bible say about lying?" The seven-year old scrambled Scripture *"A lie is an abomination unto the Lord and a very present help in time of trouble."* However, "a lie" in golf can be in the fairway or the rough, but in life a lie always lands you in the rough of Satan's bunker.

People are out on the broken limb of materialism (verse 2)

Money was this little man's big problem. A survey asked people about their dreams and what amount they needed to fulfill them. Wendy Tokuda, a TV news anchorwoman in L.A., said, "Ten million dollars, just for breathing room." Zaccheus had become wealthy but with a bad conscious and an empty life. In that same survey, a baker, Kristen Gingretch of Virginia, said that she just needed $1,000. "We are Mennonite Christians. I would use the money to buy a few personal things, some shoes, and clothes. The rest I would send to missionaries working in the field." She has discovered contentment and the simplicity of true success. Stuff can't fill the void; the more you get, the more you want. The more Zaccheus ripped off others, the more let down he felt in frustration.

People are also out on the broken limb of waffling (verse 2)

Zaccheus had displayed a lack of loyalty to his own country by becoming a pawn of the Romans. Like many Americans, he earlier wanted to keep his options open by not getting tied down. His life was on the auction block for the highest bidder. Most today run from "pledges" as if they host swine flu. Most resist systematic giving as rigid, formal, and limiting rather than seeing the freedom in disciplined commitment.

Someone expressed true "integrity" by this verbal commitment, "I will do exactly what I say I will do when I say I will do it. If I change my mind, I will tell you in advance so that you will not be harmed by my actions." Integrity integrates your life. It only comes from a commitment to get out on a limb. Meeting Christ, Zaccheus' life suddenly changed. He immediately made a verbal commitment to fly the flag and burn the bridges, letting everyone know where he stood.

We Must Get Out On A Limb With Jesus

We need a life-changing appointment (verse 5)

Jesus knows the "trees" where we are perched. He saw this guy peering through the leaves and knew his name. In the gospels, on eight occasions, Jesus accepted an invitation to dinner. But this is the only time when Jesus invited Himself over to someone's house. The King of the universe stands at the door and knocks (Rev. 3:20). If you "*hear His voice, open the door*" and come down from the tree. He will "*receive you gladly*" (verse 6).

In verse 5, Luke uses one of his favorite words, "today," which conveys the present fulfillment of God's plan of salvation, as in verse 9. Jesus "must stay" at the publican's house (verse 5). This is a divine imperative and opportunity for fullness instead of emptiness. When Christ "settles down and makes Himself permanently at home in you" (the literal idea of Ephesians 3:17), then He is free to do what He pleases with your time, talents, and treasures. Today, right now, surrender control of all that you have to Him.

Non-believers are quick to criticize Christianity as sentimental or impractical. If it is impractical, it is our fault and not the Gospel's. As soon as Zaccheus hit the ground, the Lordship of Christ became effective. Someone observed that fish swim in schools, but they don't go to school to learn to swim. Through Christ's salvation, your nature changes and you want to honor Him with you and yours. It "comes naturally," or actually "supernaturally!" That's reality and sincerity, not sentimentality. His way will work if you let Him do it His way.

We make a life-changing divestment (verse 8)

Zaccheus immediately gave 50% of everything he had to the poor. Then he pledged in restitution four times the amount of what he had extorted from the people. He said, "*I give*" (verse 8), which is best rendered, "I will give." (in the future tense). This is a statement of resolve and commitment totally unlike his earlier waffling. The check had to be written, but the money was as good as in the bank. Commitment is no longer a dirty word.

Then he said, "*If I have defrauded anyone of anything.*" This word is a first-class conditional in the New Testament Greek language that really means not "if" but "since" (since I have extorted). He was honestly confessing sin.

We do not always follow Jesus as He demanded the rich young ruler. This pledge was what God was leading Zaccheus to do at that time. Jesus told the young leader, *"Sell all that you possess and distribute it to the poor"* (Luke 18:22). God may work in your life in a different way, but an encounter with Jesus always "rattles your cage," "rocks your world," and makes you "all shook up."

Larry Thompson, pastor of the First Baptist Church of Fort Lauderdale, Florida, knew the founder of Wendy's, Dave Thomas. Occasionally, he visited the church and would call Larry, "Pope." One day he said: "Pope, I got a letter from a man who used to be in management with me twenty years ago. He wrote to tell me that he had found Jesus Christ, and he sent me $600.00 that he had cheated with when he had worked for me. Do you think if he gets a little more of Jesus he will send me the interest?" Unlike that employee, Zaccheus was certainly operating in his new life with much interest on his debt.

Zaccheus gave half of his goods in a known amount. Then he spoke of an unknown amount that God would reveal to him (verse 8). Financial giving to the Lord through His church should involve regular, systematic tithing and also spontaneous giving, which you do not plan for in advance. He will teach you (Ps. 34:8) – what, where, and how to give. It may mean getting out on a limb in faith. I can testify that He will lift you up and not let you down. Make sure that you are clinging to His limb.

Zaccheus was no longer me-centered but others-oriented. He was concerned for "the poor" and those he had "defrauded." It then affected his whole family. *"Salvation came to his house"* (verse 9). Faith-based giving will involve all of your family. The blessings always spill over. Your family should also pray with you about your giving. Your surrender might be used by God to bring about their salvation.

We make a life-long investment (verse 8)

Take a long look. A man of means gave thousands of dollars to build mission churches but later lost his wealth in a financial downturn. A friend who knew of his gifts to Christian work asked: "Don't you wish that you had not given all that money to build those churches? If you had not given that money, you would still have enough to start over." But the wise Christian who understood building an eternal portfolio replied, "The money I gave is all that I saved. If I had not given it, I would have lost that too."

Your Investment Involves Following Biblical Principles

The late great preacher, Adrian Rogers, gave me insight about this over the phone as I prepared to teach on this subject: "Hayes, don't forget to teach these principles. They will change your church." God also spoke through him to my heart.

God owns everything and expects us to examine our lives

Dr. Rogers then told me how the wise men brought gold, frankincense and myrrh to baby Jesus. The gold pictures dominion. All wealth belongs to the Sovereign King. Incense speaks of worship, which belongs to Jesus as our Lord. The myrrh, used for embalming dead bodies, speaks of His sacrifice. Jesus is our Savior, and I must witness for Him. Therefore, you have to ask yourself, just as Adrian asked me:

- Is there anything that I will not give to God if He desires it? If there is, then I am covetous.

- Is there anything that I love, fear, or serve more than Jesus? If there is, then I am idolatrous.

- Is there any person that I will not speak to in witness? If so, then I am rebellious.

God allows us to use His resources and expects us to impact our world

We participate in giving. [I am going to walk down into the audience with two one hundred dollar bills, and I am going to give them to two people.] "This is yours. I am giving it to you for you to hold. Don't run out and spend it. Now since I gave it, I can ask for it back. Okay, I want it back! If I gave it to you to buy a hamburger and also buy one for a poor person in the street, then you would use it out of my resources which I have given to you. I am giving you (another person) a bill to give back in the offering later in the service. I'll trust you to do it." This pictures the way God gives to us and He often leads us to distribute His wealth, even as we meet our own obligations. He owns everything!

God commands us to acknowledge His provision and expects us to tithe regularly of our income

Zaccheus was called "*a son of Abraham*" by Jesus (verse 9). Abraham gave 10% to the Priest of Salem named Melchizedek (Gen. 14:18-24). Tithing was not invented by Baptists. Next to prayer, it is the oldest practice of God's people. Five hundred years before any book of the Bible was written, a man tithed. Sixteen hundred years before, Malachi 3 records God's words about tithing to "*the storehouse,*" we find the first tither in the Bible. It also mentions the first priest, not after the order of Aaron, but a royal priest after the order of Melchizedek.

Who was this mysterious man? He was "*without father and without mother*" (Heb. 7:3). Could it be that this was a pre-incarnate appearance of Jesus in the Old Testament? The two offices of king and priest were never combined in Israel until Jesus came. He administered the bread and wine, which speaks of the sufferings of Christ as pictured in the Lord's Supper. In John 8:56 Jesus said yet Abraham *rejoiced to see his day*. He was certainly a type of Christ

(Heb. 7:3).

After Abraham rescued his nephew, Lot, from pagan kings, he tithed of their spoil. It was there that Abraham learned a new name for God who is *the Most High, Possessor of heaven and earth*" (Gen. 14:19). He thus tithed out of his worship experience, just as we must today. Truly we say, "Blessed be God Most High" as we give "*a tenth of all*" (Gen. 14:19, 20). The tithe should never be out of duty but out of love. It is the starting point but not the stopping place of joyful giving to God and His work. Abraham was *blessed* by God (Gen. 14:19). This speaks of joy as well as favor. It blesses us as well as God when we give. Indeed, "*It is more blessed to give than to receive*" (Acts 20:35).

Melchidezek was not God's IRS agent. He did not assess Abraham. Those who mistake tithing as part of the law may not understand this passage. He was grateful for God's "*deliverance*" (Gen. 14:20), just as Zaccheus rejoiced in his salvation.

Though we give at least a tithe (ten percent) of our income just like Abraham, we are to demonstrate "grace giving" (2 Cor. 9:8). The world is impressed by the Gates Foundation gift of $35 billion to charity. Yet King David said, "*Now with all my ability I have provided for the house of my God...*" (1 Chron. 29:2).

My businessman friend, Kirk Hintz estimated the current value of his gifts of gold. As of the writing of this message, the current gold price per troy ounce equals $1,317.00. Since David gave 100,000 talents of gold, that equals $144,015,118,100.08! Wow, what generosity! How can we New Testament saints be stingy? How can we be satisfied with just the bare minimum? Compared to David, how can we think we are such "hot stuff" about giving our stuff? Yet, we must start somewhere, climbing up the tree, crawling out on ever-higher branches, beginning with ten percent.

A wealthy man became obsessed in his old age with the idea that something was wrong with his hands. "Look at them. They are so empty. I have spent my life amassing what I could hold, and now there is nothing to show for it." It is not too late for you to give your hands and what they hold to God. They can either be a clenched fist or open palms. Today, get out on a limb in faith and obedience.

11

Godly Wisdom for Financial Freedom
PROVERBS 21:20
Michael C. Catt
President of 2008 Pastors' Conference

*"The wise person saves for the future,
but the foolish person spends all he gets."*

– Proverbs 21:20

Solomon covers the whole spectrum of finances in the book of Proverbs:
- Getting money
- Investing
- Spending
- Squandering
- Loaning
- Giving

The average American middle class couple is living off 120% of their income. In other words, they are one extended sickness, tragedy, crisis, or lay-off from disaster! Someone said, "Money isn't everything, but it does give your children a reason to call." Money brings out the best and worst in people. Nothing causes more stress in a person's life or conflict in a marriage than running out of money before running out of month. One man said, "I am driven by two things: love and fear. The love of money and the fear of going broke."

God is interested in *how* you spend the hours of your life and *where* you will spend eternity. Proverbs was not written to impress the rich or discourage the poor. It does not condemn those who are rich when they handle their wealth wisely, nor does it teach that being poor is shameful.

Why Should I Honor The Lord With My Money?

"Where your treasure is, there will your heart be also." – Matthew 6:21 (NASB)

This verse also applies in the reverse: Your money will follow the affections of your heart.

What is it about your money management that embarrasses or frustrates you? This is something you need to get a handle on. Over the course of your life, if you keep a job, you're going to handle a significant amount of money. What will you have to show for it? What will you have invested in?

What does the Bible say about our money?

I am to honor the Lord with it

"Honor the Lord from your wealth" – Proverbs 3:9 (NIV)

Those who honor God with what they have are blessed in return. "Honor" means to esteem greatly or to worship. Why does this matter? Because the Lord gives us the ability and talents to produce wealth. According to Proverbs 22:2, He is the maker of the rich and the poor.

Money is an extension of who I am. You can tell a lot about a person by how they spend their money:
* Likes and dislikes
* Value system
* Feelings toward God, family, and others
* Recreation, entertainment
* The importance of housing, clothes, cars, vacations, etc.
* Mindset toward saving

- Good/poor stewardship (credit report, overdrafts, late notices, etc.)

I am accountable to God for how I spend it

Some may say, "I earned it. I'll do what I want with it." But if God hadn't given you the ability, talents, and gifts, you wouldn't be where you are today.

Money management is part of my relationship with Christ

If He is my Lord, my money can't be off limits. Christianity is more than praying, reading the Bible, and going to church. The Bible gives us a holistic view of what it means to be a Christian. Our lives are not compartmentalized. The mind of Christ is to permeate our parenting, relationships, politics, work ethic, and so on. Wisdom gives guidance to wealth and helps us determine how to give, spend, and invest.

"Since riches never made anyone honest or generous or discerning, wisdom must come aboard to steer us away from disaster." – Chuck Swindoll

You cannot be a Christian leader if you can't manage your own household

Money is static–there's no magic in it. The Bible teaches that if you are going to be a leader (i.e., pastor, minister, deacon, etc.) you've got to manage your financial house well. You'll never find financial freedom if you don't get a plan for your life. Think of it this way: you trade part of your life away for money. If you earn $10 per hour and you buy an $800 couch, you've traded 80 hours of your life for that couch.

How Can I Honor The Lord With My Money?

"Money is in some respects like fire; it is a very excellent servant, but a terrible master." – P. T. Barnum

Unfortunately, money is the master in many homes. It dominates discussions and creates tension, stress, and anxiety. It is often cited as the reason behind a divorce. We look for the first and fifteenth of the month like a squirrel looking for nuts.

America is consumed with "Who Wants to Be a Millionaire" and a dozen other "get rich quick" spin-off shows. I've never met anyone who didn't want to be a millionaire. There's nothing wrong with being one, but the key is how you get there.

I honor the Lord in the way I get it

Honorable:

- I can inherit it. (Prov. 19:14)
- I can work for it. (Prov. 10:4; 12:11, 24, 27; 13:4; 21:25, 26; 29:19)

Dishonorable:

- I can take a bribe. (Prov. 15:27; 17:23; 21:14)
- I can steal it. (Prov. 13:11; 28:24; Ephesians 4:28)
- I can use a get-rich-quick scheme. (Prov. 28:20)
- I can gamble. (11% of people surveyed by Money Magazine said the best way to get rich is to play the lottery. People think, "The next roll of the dice or the next ticket and all my problems will be over.")

I honor the Lord in my attitude toward getting it

- It requires discernment. (Prov. 30:8)
- It requires diligence. (Prov. 10:4)
- It requires discipline. (Prov. 13:11)

I honor the Lord in my disbursement of it

- The first 10% goes to God (Prov. 3:9). This demonstrates trust. Each time the Bible mentions tithing (see Mal. 3:8-10), it speaks of a blessing to follow. God says, "You do this, and I'll honor you back!"

- The second 10% goes to savings. Pay yourself, invest, save. This isn't mad money to spend foolishly; this is for your future.
- The remaining 80% goes to everything else.

I heard about an evangelist who was preaching to a cheap church. He preached hard on money, hoping he could soften their hearts. When the message was over, the deacons told him to pass his hat because they didn't have offering plates in the church. When the hat had been passed, there wasn't one thin dime in it. The evangelist bowed his head and said, "Let's pause now to give thanks." As they bowed, the congregation wondered what in the world the man had to be thankful for. He prayed, "Lord, I'm just so thankful I got my hat back!"

When all is said and done, your financial condition is a moral, spiritual, and character issue. What would your life look like on the 10/10/80 plan? Think about it:

- A 25-year-old makes $15,000 a year with no raises for 20 years. On this plan, by age 45 he or she would have given over $30,000 to God's work, put $30,000 into a mutual fund, and built a nest egg worth more than $85,000.
- A 40-year-old makes $60,000 a year with no raises for 20 years. On this plan, by age 60 he or she would have given $120,000 to God's work, established at least $343,000 in investments, and have the rest to live off of.
- But you can't do this if you're living off 120% of your income!

How Can I Honor The Lord In The Way I Spend My Money?

Establish sound principles
- Don't buy what you can't afford. (Prov. 23:5)
- Don't borrow what you can't repay. (Prov. 22:7)
- Don't guarantee what you don't have. (Prov. 6:1ff)

Avoid the mistakes of others

When you look at people who have made a mess of their lives, you see they failed to invest in anything eternal. They live in financial bondage and fall into one of these traps because they don't have a plan.

- **Impulsive Spending:** They walk through a store and buy when they see a sale. They take advantage of prequalified credit cards and no-down-payment deals.

- **Compulsive Spending:** Spending becomes an escape mechanism to feel better about themselves or their circumstances, and they end up in bondage to their shopping.

- **Revenge Spending:** They get mad about their financial situation, and envy or jealousy causes them to blow their money while they try to prove a point.

- **Boredom Spending:** If you have extra time on your hands, quit going to the mall and go do something constructive.

- **Special Interest Spending:** This type of spending focuses on a hobby. While they may use discretion in every other area, here caution is thrown to the wind.

- **Status Spending:** Don't spend your future or your health trying to keep up with someone else. Let the Lord set you free from trying to keep up with the Joneses.

Here's a little lesson to help you. Use it with your kids! Show your child a $5 bill in your wallet. Then show him a credit card and tell him it has a $5,000 limit. Ask the question, "How much money do I have to spend?" If he answers, "$5,005," it's time to have a discussion about reality. If he answers, "You still have $5," you may want to consider turning your finances over to your child.

"How blessed is the man who finds wisdom and the man who gains understanding. For her profit is better than the profit of silver and her gain better than fine gold. She is more precious than jewels; and nothing you desire compares with her." – Proverbs 3:13-15 (NASB)